THE HIGH JUMP

THE HIGH JUMP

A NEW ZEALAND CHILDHOOD

ELIZABETH KNOX

VICTORIA UNIVERSITY PRESS

VICTORIA UNIVERSITY PRESS
Victoria University of Wellington
PO Box 600 Wellington

ISBN 0 86473 337 2

First published in slightly different form:
Paremata © 1989
Pomare © 1994
Tawa © 1998

This edition first published 2000

The author gratefully acknowledges the assistance
of the ICI Writers Bursary and project grants from
the QEII Arts Council and Creative NZ
in writing the parts of this book

Printed by PrintLink, Wellington

TO MY FIRST FAMILY:

RAY AND HEATHER, MARY AND SARA

AND MY SECOND FAMILY:

FERGUS AND JACK

Contents

POMARE   9

PAREMATA   79

TAWA   161

Afterword   269

POMARE

1

The children found a stand of poisonous berries beside the metal footbridge that spanned the Hutt line. 'King Edward berries,' Hayley Moynihan told her friends, Jo and Lex Keene. 'Daddy says they'll kill you.'

To ten-year-old Jo she seemed to be offering death as a delicacy. Here was an opportunity for a more extravagant 'crime' than her latest plan – saving or stealing Hori's new litter before Mr Moynihan made good his threat to put the kittens in a sack and throw them in the river. Jo stripped a branch from the bush and held it to the seven-year-olds' faces. She asked, 'Shall we eat one?'

It was a grey day, and chilly; as Hayley considered the proposition she buttoned her cardigan. The cardigan had belonged to an older cousin, its cuffs were turned up twice, it was pink and didn't suit Hayley. Very little did. Jo and Lex's mother sometimes thought *she* could make a better job of dressing the freckled redhead. Every other mother would put her girls in fashionable flounces, taffetas and gauzes, and Hayley's best dress was of turquoise crepe with white lace – very modish – but Hayley needed crisp green or blue cotton, plain, because her complexion was patterned. Hester Keene dressed her own girls in simple linen, or brown and white seersucker, or tartan skirts and jerseys in winter. And she cut their hair short.

Lex thought Hayley beautiful. At fifteen, twenty, thirty, Lex would say, 'I have a thing about red hair,' her 'thing' the result of how carefully she would watch her friend deliberate on her suggestions, to accept smiling, or reject with a quick cloudburst of blood and temper.

'Suicide is a crime,' Jo said dreamily. A crime that would put an end to all Jo's other experiments.

Hayley said, 'I don't want to be dead. Or even sick.'

'Aren't we going to feed Mercy and Playtime?' Lex asked.

Jo picked a berry and pinched it, she spread the pulp on her fingertips, seeds in their wet cauls of flesh. She put her hand to her nose – smelled poison, pungent and unappetising. This was a crime she wouldn't acquire: trespass, wagging, theft, rudies (better not to think of that), torture – but not suicide.

'And there's the election next Saturday,' Lex said, still presenting arguments.

'What's a lection?' Hayley asked.

'Grown-ups vote who's going to be Prime Minister,' Jo

explained. 'There's National and Labour – that's the best – and Social Credit. Naomi Arapa says her mother and father vote Social Credit. It happens at the school next Saturday.'

Jo threw the stem of nightshade, which struck up a spicy scent from the hedge. The three children walked on. As if responding to the tardy pull-starter of a motor mower on the far side of the hedge, the sun came out and idled weakly behind a screen of high cloud.

When they stepped onto the metal stairway of the bridge it rang and trembled. Hayley stopped. 'I'm not allowed to cross the tracks.'

'That's what the bridge is for, silly.'

Hayley rattled back down. 'See you later.' She ran along the hedge-lined path. They saw her stop at the head of the right-of-way to shake the crab apple tree, shake down several red-skinned shells, scooped hollow by birds.

In the centre of the bridge Lex and Jo stopped to check the lines in either direction. They liked to wait and look down on the ferrous, blistered tops of the units. The stretch of line to Taita, and the one to the rail bridge, river and Silverstream, were both empty – four bright channels and a tributary of sidings by a ditch of dusty blackberry.

The horses were kept in a wedge-shaped paddock by the rail line. The girls bent to pull the grass on their side of the fence and the mare, Mercy, ambled over. She thudded to a stop, huffed and scratched her chin on the top wire before lipping the grass from Jo's flat palm. Jo laughed as the whiskery lips tickled her. Playtime, the yearling, was slower to take his cue and put on a performance of fear – high-stepped over with his head swung side on, neck arched and eye rolling. Lex offered a brush of grass; he forgot his act and bit at her hand, his teeth a sprung trap. Lex flinched. Playtime lost half the grass and his mother lipped up the few strands draped over the wire. Then both animals turned their heads and stilled their jaws to sniff and listen. Lex stroked Playtime's neck, hair smooth over a wave of muscle.

Lex would say she loved horses. Her mother had taught her that song: 'Horses, horses, I love horses, white and dapple-grey . . .' In the first term she made a horse in her weekly sewing class, a stuffed horse, in silhouette, two-legged, his nose oddly rounded. She had sketched her pattern on newspaper and pinned it to a doubled-over swatch of gingham – green and white chequered cotton poplin. She cut her horse out, tacked his outline, then carefully restitched in close, neat blanket-stitch. But when she turned him right way out Lex forgot to poke the stuffing – strips of her mother's old stockings – deep into his snout. In consequence he had, at first, a pouch mouth she could fasten to her nose or fingers. She gave her horse a bright pink wool mane and tail, black eyes and no saddle. 'It's a brumby, a mustang,' she told her sewing teacher. She had just earned library privileges and had slipped a shelf over into the nine to twelve-year-old section. This was a wild Walter Farley, Mary O'Hara horse. She named him Sweetpea, but he became Horsey.

Horsey was her sole toy talisman. A loved and grubby toy, the kind most children acquire in infancy, to cherish and grieve for when absent for even one night. Lex did that. Horsey was ill-advisedly washed on a day when clouds stood at the lip of the hills and the wind changed. Lex checked the warming cupboard every half hour to see whether Horsey was dry and they could both go to bed.

14

She couldn't sleep without him wedged into her left palm. Yet Lex had made Horsey, and had had no particular loyalty to a toy before that time. She slept with Horsey for ten years. Perhaps it was at seven that she began banking on dreams, on things she had made; from then was condemned to stand outside the gates of the Holy City, when the world has ended, with dogs and sorcerers, and whoremongers, and murderers, and idolaters, and *those who make and love lies*. At thirty she had Horsey still. He was coated with acidic grime; her ancient sleep-sweat had corroded his skin in brittle-edged holes, like cigarette burns. Skin? Skins. The first, green and white gingham; then, at ten, a smaller check in blue and white; then brown and white plaid at twelve; and at sixteen a final cover, very colourful, a white wool mane and cursory black cotton eye (a blurred black star that the writer brightens with ink).

Jo didn't take to sewing. Early in the year Mr Heron, an energetic teacher, a man with a shelf of books on educational theory, became worried about Jo Keene. Jo's mind wandered, she was slow in responding to questions, wouldn't do some things, took no pleasure in reciting her nine-times table. The infant mistress had always called Jo 'dreamboat', she thought Jo fey, but the conscientious Mr Heron, trying to do well by his entire class of forty-two, booked Jo in for a psychological appraisal. Jo took a letter home to her parents. Frank Keene combed his black hair up into a swollen wattle. 'Who do they think they are? *Psychology!* I don't believe in it. Mumbo-jumbo as a tool of the State. Anyway, who *wants* a normal child?' Jo was frightened by this reaction; they – the school – must think she was nuts.

She was interviewed in the staffroom. It proved fun. Teachers ducked in and out, fetching things and apologising to both her interviewer and to *her*. Pretty, perfumed young women teachers saying 'sorry' to Jo. Her chair was comfortable and she enjoyed the psychologist's puzzles, his patter, his clock with a second hand. She took his searching questions about her family as permission to interrogate him about his wife and children. As the infant mistress said later to Hester Keene, 'When I popped in Jo was grilling the poor man.'

Jo had no learning disorder, Mr Heron reported to Hester, in fact she was possibly the brightest child in the school. Perhaps she would rather take model-making with the boys than sewing with the girls? Jo made a papier-mâché dinosaur, a balsa wood aeroplane, and a cardboard speedboat painted with high-gloss enamel and varnish, so that she could float it in the paddling pool at home. Lex, at seven, her first year of sewing, made Horsey.

Thomas Sand stood at the fence, waiting to waylay any children who passed along the right-of-way to Taita Drive. Under his arm he held an enamel basin full of fresh peas his mother had given him to pod for tea. His classmate Jo Keene and her little sister Lex stopped and leaned on the fence; the wire squawked and gave. They took some of his peas, popping and splitting the pods, prising out the odds and evens with their tongues. Thomas listened to all they had to say – about the bridge and Hayley turning tail, the King Edward berries, Mercy and Playtime. He told his own news: another gift, Mother's sponge cake, a phone call from an aunt in England to whom he'd been allowed to speak –

all the things he had done during today's period of house arrest.

Thomas noticed everything, and reported in a soft, unhurried voice. His eyes were sleepy, his hair fair and sparse and his skin, like Hester's camellias, milky and prone to rusty bruises. He had been sick for some time. In the spring his hair fell out and he wore a knitted hat, like a tea cosy; it covered his scalp and conserved his heat. Thomas had two older sisters, one already at High. His father was a chauffeur and had driven the Daimler the Queen rode in on her last visit. Mr and Mrs Sand were from England.

Thomas's oldest sister, Glenda, came over. She took the basin from him. 'Mum will need the remainder of these.' Jo and Lex hid their pea pods behind their backs.

'Did you eat many?' Glenda asked her brother. When Thomas said he had she looked pleased.

It was lunchtime, so Jo ran on up Taita Drive while Lex took time to tuck her dress into her panties and execute a forward roll over the bars at the head of the right-of-way.

Hester asked, 'Why don't you eat the rest of your egg?'

'The remainder of my egg?' Lex asked, seeing how Glenda's word worked.

'Yes. What's left.'

Lex thoughtfully scooped the scrambled egg to the left side of her plate and was told not to play with her food. Her mother negotiated three more mouthfuls in exchange for Lex's drink. Lex renegotiated two if she had to put on her pinafore.

Jo, Lex and four-year-old Steph went down to the shed in the back garden, sucking their lemon and barley-water out of Cerebos sauce bottles. Jo's and Steph's had been soy bottles and had only a single hole in their lids. Jo could tip hers out in a stream onto her tongue – the way Spaniards drink wine from goatskins, she told her sisters. She had seen a film at school. Lex's bottle had five holes in its lid and drizzled. She liked to stopper the liquid with her tongue, feel five discrete, cool dimples, then a flood like the spit of hunger.

The shed was covered in honeysuckle and stood right up against the boundary fence of a house on Molesworth Street. Jo and Lex used to climb from the fence onto the shed roof and then jump off; Jo because it was a challenge, safe without any audience but her little sisters. At school Jo always ducked the softball and trailed in last in races. Yet only she and Naomi Arapa, of all the neighbourhood, would scale the parapets of old blackberry that grew over the felled willows on the river bank. If she did choose to catch the softball it wouldn't be to please Miss Patterson, who went on about sportsmanship and team spirit but abused any child who flinched, lagged, or lost. Jo never felt inept under the gaze of the dark compound eyes of in-accessible berries.

Whenever Lex jumped off the shed roof she thought she would fly, not fall. She dreamed of flying, of picking up her feet to bob at the corner of the kitchen, against the ceiling. Or she soared, dodging pylons and high tension wires, under the shadows of zeppelins or over seas of whales – long eerie shadows, like the swarms of wardrobe monsters that had kept her awake and watchful in her infancy. Or perhaps the shadows were like Jo's smelly, nebulous, ballooning 'pardies' – as the girls were taught to say when they farted, 'Pardon me' childishly commuted. Jo had described how a fart would look and behave, and Lex would still swear sometimes she could see them, like several of Jo's other inventions, invisible by daylight. Lex dreamed of flying, so after breakfast would climb onto the shed roof and leap off, looking out and up, rather than down, sure that *this time* she would be snatched upward.

Jo checked her tadpoles, in their plastic bucket filled with stones and duckweed. Little John's and Mayflower's legs had emerged from the buds by their tails; Big John's were longer and his eyes seemed to be moving towards the top of his head.

Steph found an old peach stone in the garden. She had Lex split it open for her on the path to the clothesline and then ate its shrivelled kernel. Like her sisters Steph was a keen forager. She didn't have their discernment, however, and sometimes ate things that made her sick.

Her younger sister's grubbing reminded Lex to disinter the dolls. She fetched her spade from the apple box in the back porch and first dug up the papier-mâché doll Jo had made and they had buried, in a shoebox coffin and with due ceremony, some weeks before. It was the second time he'd been dug up and he was becoming quite corpse-like – a faded, pale pulp. His mouth and moustache had become indistinguishable and the damp had scalped him, parted his rabbit fur crew-cut and paper cranium.

Tuppence was buried in a plastic lunch box, a survival capsule, equipped with a bed, water, food stores and reading matter – one of Hester's miniature books, the suede-bound *Thoughts from Tolstoy*. This project was inspired by a newspaper headline: French Scientist Spends 52 Days Underground. The final frontier had retreated beyond the means of lone explorers, but endurance feats were all the rage: land speed records on the dry salt lakes of Utah, papyrus boats on the Pacific waves. Lex told Tuppence she had spent twenty-three days underground and had some distance yet to go. She brushed the mildew out of Tuppence's hair and resealed the lunch box.

'The girls said they saw Thomas Sand today,' said Hester.

Frank Keene had his typewriter on the kitchen table; he was knocking off an article he hadn't been able to finish at work on Friday. He had paused to think and was, as always, rubbing his palms back and forth along his thighs. His suit pants grew shiny and corded velvet bald by these deliberations. 'Do the girls understand about Thomas?' Frank asked.

'I don't know. I mean, I can't say I understand it.' Hester felt grave, but found herself smiling at the cat, who came into the kitchen, looked warily at Frank and found him acceptable seated and with slippered feet – Brindle had no objection to Frank himself but Frank's dress or heavier work shoes appalled him.

Hester poured the cat a little milk and watched with pleasure as he sat and draped his front feet with his tail. She had always loved cats. There had been several batches in her childhood. When her father was alive the cats would wait for him on the front walk of the house on Maori Hill. The family would hear him in conversation with them: 'What have you been up to? What have you got there? You rogue. Lovely puss. Lizards again? What a spot for a cat. Ah. Don't snatch, mate!' To his family he would say just,

'Hello,' and shake the paper open.

Frank was saying, 'Do you mean you don't understand because Thomas is only a child? That's a little sentimental.'

'*Everybody* feels that way. And it's worse if you have children of your own.'

'Ours are healthy.'

'Look. I was as frightened by Steph's bronchitis as by your rushed appendix job. Poor Mrs Sand, it's like lightning striking.'

Frank finished his sentence and lit another cigarette. He wondered if he'd ever told Hester his lightning story.

'And Jo says he's the nicest boy. It's true. Possibly the illness has made him gentler and more thoughtful. He's a little girlish. His mother taught him French knitting so he'd have something else to do in bed. When he's up he walks about trailing his knitting.' Hester picked up the cat, who gave an alarming wet belch. She said, 'Sometimes it does seem true – that the good die young. Or the sweet, anyway.'

Frank remembered the dim front room of his childhood home, the white gloom of lace curtains, women in rusty black wool, taffeta, velvet, jet – and that supposed comforting commonplace: Suffer the little children.

'Think of Paul,' Hester said.

Paul, son of Hester's landlady, Frank's friend, was sweet-natured, not just friendly or pleasant, but good. Frank and Paul had gone walking on the lower slopes of Egmont in the spring, several months before Paul's nephritis finally killed him. Frank couldn't recall their conversation. He did remember a deer trail, the punctured, crusty snow, then a yellow trench of urine, steaming, a flurry on the bank above them and the stag looking back across its flank, red hide softened through a haze of its own breath, and frost in its eyelashes. And Frank remembered how he took the wheel on the way home, while Paul slept in the back seat. Paul was spent and pale. On the Himatangi straight the wind buffeted the little Austin. Frank fought to hold it steady. Dark night, deep sleep, rough ride – Paul might have been one of Frank's children, the way he felt.

Frank said, 'Have I ever told you about the lightning?'

Frank and another alpine guide had set out to carry supplies to a party of climbers stranded at Ball Hut. The road was snowed in and there was no getting a tractor through. Frank's partner carried a pack of food; Frank had a six-gallon drum of kerosene strapped to his back, which gurgled in a distinctly spiritous way at his every step.

The ceiling of cloud was low, snow on the slope to the left of the road loose and threatening. Mist moved now and then between the men and their view below and behind of that white and preposterously wide road, the Tasman Glacier.

They heard the storm coming up the far side of Sefton, closer, sharp concussions of thunder then the bass chorus of an avalanche shaken loose in the opposite valley. The men stopped. The tin on Frank's back boomed. A small snowfall skidded down the slope above the road just in front of the guides. Frank's partner went ahead to take a look, first shrugging off the pack so that, if he must, he could make a quick retreat. His ice axe was still fastened to the top of his pack. Frank thrust the spike on his axe-handle into the snow, and used the head to rest on, like a hacking-cane. For a moment it was quiet, but for the creak of their feet in the snow. Then, beneath Frank's hand, his ice axe began to hum. He raised it, broke contact with the ground, but it went on vibrating like a tuning fork. Something was on its way, something unlike anything he knew – the jolts he'd heard when he put his ear to a railway line in a quiet landscape, or, his head underwater, the sound of the prop of a big ship coming into the bay. Frank flung the ice axe from him. It sailed out over the glacier and was struck by lightning. Only a thin capillary of electricity, but around the two men the air was instantly solid, deafening, and as brassy as small change.

They went on, with supplies to deliver. But on the way back the following morning, in finer weather, they climbed down from the road onto the glacier to look for the axe. And found a comma-shaped hole milled from the ice where the axe-head had melted its way down into the glacier, too deep for sight.

Lex met Hayley riding her trike along the footpath by the Keenes'. Hayley wore a blue brocade dress of her mother's – a discarded ballroom-dancing dress, eight years out of date, with a spangly train that trailed behind her along the concrete, catching. Its glitter fidgeted. Hayley showed Lex a small gilt box that held her mother's lipstick. She'd pinched it. The lipstick was sweating, a waxy red. The girls scooped some out with their fingers and rubbed it in, lip to lip, as they had seen their mothers do. It made Lex's throat catch, as if she'd been sucking on a crayon. Hayley bundled her train into the tray of her trike. Lex got in and Hayley dubbed her up the street.

On top of the stopbank some big boys were sky-lining like television Apaches. They had found the corpse of a large dead rat and took turns swinging it about by its tail. One saw Lex and Hayley, and spun in a circle to hammertoss the rat at them. It landed with a smack on the path behind the girls. Hayley pedalled quickly into the Sands' front yard. The boys stood watching them for a moment then dropped out of sight on the far side of the bank. Two of the boys were Hayley's brothers, twins, high-school boys and members of the gang that by report had built a pit fort over the stopbank. A deep pit, round as an octopus's head with eight tunnels for tentacles, it was roofed with corrugated iron and camouflaged with cut willow branches and broom.

'Shall we follow them?' Hayley asked, then bent over to prise at the pennies Mr Sand had set into the drive. Every child tried in passing, but the pennies had withstood all assaults, even those of mad David Hough with his father's best screwdriver.

'Not today.' Lex could hear her older sister's voice behind the Sands' house. She got off the tray of the trike and waved to Hayley who pedalled on.

The Sand girls and Jo were playing darts. Thomas watched from the back steps. He was wearing plaid slippers and a duffel coat over his summer shirt and shorts. He was keeping score.

They let Lex join, then scoffed as her darts rebounded from the wire web on the board's face or sank themselves into the lawn behind the rotary clothesline – the board hung from the hook for the peg basket. Even Glenda, the sixteen-year-old, failed to say, 'Give her a chance, she's only young,' but, 'You little clot! It's just a flick of the wrist!' Jo was no good at it either, but was improving – besides, *she'd* been invited. Glenda threw wide once, her younger sister jeered and Thomas called out *not* to run around behind the board while Lex was taking her turn, then, 'Not yet, Lex!'

Lex threw very wide – or her eyes strayed from the board and she was looking down the shaft of plastic-fletched brass at Glenda beyond the clothesline stooping to retrieve her dart. Lex threw and her dart sank into Glenda's ankle. Glenda sat down, the dart drooped and a line of blood trickled down into Glenda's shoe. Lex dropped her other darts and ran.

She was sure she *had* aimed at Glenda, but never believed she would hit her mark. Anyway, the injury would look like an accident. She had made an impact; with Glenda's cry of pain, wilt, huddle, Lex had solidified. She was a *big* clot, a choking clot of thrombosis, a lethal, considerable clot.

The villain and fugitive ran across Taita Drive and scrambled up the stopbank. Last winter the council had built the bank up a little along that stretch of the river and the top was still furrowed and cross-hatched by bulldozer tracks. When the bulldozers had done, the council sprayed the bank with some substance that formed a gritty white scab then sprouted clover. Lex lay stomach down in the thick clover on the far slope. Across the summit of the bank she watched Jo leave Sands', look both ways along the road, then walk home.

It was Thomas who pulled the spike from Glenda's ankle. His other sister, Jenny, ran indoors to fetch their mum. Jo

Keene said, 'I'd better be going.' She held her arms as if it were cold and her cardie out at its elbows. Glenda's eyes watered, but she wouldn't shed tears over an injury inflicted by a little kid. Mrs Sand hurried out and Jo Keene backed away around the corner of the house.

Thomas's mum said he was a good boy and not to linger outside and catch a chill. She helped Glenda to her feet and supported her up the back steps.

Thomas wasn't tough, like the boys who kept on fighting, even with bloodied noses; he just wasn't squeamish. When his sisters' budgie escaped its cage and got its leg entangled in the fishing line of a home-made mobile, and the Sand children found it, upside down, fluttering and shrieking, the girls pressed their hands to their cheeks and cried. But Thomas cut it down and held it quiet while he unwound turn after turn of the nylon thread sunk into the swollen flesh of its leg.

For Thomas was patient, and his patience gave him the substance to stay upright in the pressure waves of others' pain. It was easy if you could see the cause – steel spike or constricting thread – to do something to kick the wedges out from the wheels of *that* life, to get it rolling again. Blood would flow freely, then the wound close.

Thomas had thought that way of his own suffering and spells in bed. They were an interruption, static, a break in transmission. But then – there was something he saw on TV, when his headache hadn't let him sleep and Dad had bundled him up in candlewick and sat him between them on the settee. Mum and Dad. They were there, so he dozed. They were watching some drama, a grown-up programme, and Thomas heard the wise-old-woman character say that someone was 'young and unfinished'. He stored the phrase away. It was an illumination as vivid as his dreams of being younger and running, running not yet breathless along a colonnade of trees, in his strength, under sunlit leaves, great thunderclaps of green.

Jo Keene, who was his age – but his birthday was earlier in the year – was the cleverest girl Thomas knew. Jo had showed him a book she'd been writing: *Honey and John on Windy Hill*. She knew about Beethoven's deafness, and that Zeus and Jupiter were the same god by different names. But Jo was unfinished. Nobody stared at her the way they would stare at Thomas (the way he'd peer into his own reflection) to see the thing that would one day leap out from behind his image and engulf it, like the scorched then fire-holed map of the Ponderosa at the beginning of *Bonanza*.

At dusk, when the sun had skipped along the top of the hills, touched three crests, then finally gone down, Frank came along Taita Drive from his Saturday evening walk to the dairy. Every Saturday, while the roast was cooking, he went for ice-cream cones and Hester's weekly bar of white chocolate.

As Frank turned in at his letterbox he saw his middle daughter, further along the road, sitting with her feet in the gutter. The lower half of Lex's face was red. Wind-chapped, Frank assumed; a rare November southerly had set in. Lex had found a sea shell and was holding it up to her ear. Where had she acquired that bit of whimsy? He must explain acoustics to her some time.

*

Lex had found the shell in the gutter by Arapas', bulky and brown among the empty halves of flat, white tuatua. It was warm in her hand, had a rim like a helmet and a spiral dome. She held it to her ear to hear the sea and it kissed her, a warm wet kiss. She touched her ear. Stickiness. It spilled from the shell onto her fingers, a curdled, olive-green slime that stank and seethed. Lex dropped the shell. She retched, but caught the bile in her mouth and swallowed.

She washed at the outside tap under the lounge windows, where Hester had planted pinks and carnations between the brown topknots of exhausted iris leaves. Both the rot and remains of lipstick were greasy and stubborn; grease sealed her skin like Vaseline so the water formed blisters on it. She went indoors to try soap.

In the lounge Steph and Jo were watching The NZBC Report, footage of the Gemini Twelve splash-down. It had been in the newspaper three days before, without pictures; Naomi had brought the item to school for current events. Mr Heron put 'gravity' and 'vacuum' on Standard Four's spelling list. James Lovell and 'Buzz' Aldrin stood on the foredeck of a battleship, waving, and smiling through their beards. 'Buzz' had the new record, a five-and-a-half hour space walk. More pictures. Jo was fascinated by this puffy figure spinning on the end of its umbilicus, without inertia, making big movements from small gestures, like a god tossing in its sleep. Steph sat in her TV chair, one of the cane dining chairs. Her parents wanted to encourage her to keep her back straight. All the girls were round-shouldered. Hester would nag the older two: 'Your torso should sit on your hips like an egg in an egg-cup.'

When Lex had washed her face thoroughly she joined her sisters. Jo hadn't told on her, had reported neither her 'mistake' nor her absence. Lex wondered how long she had hidden, skulking along the far side of the stopbank, almost to the rail bridge (but she never went there alone). Perhaps no time had passed, she had dawdled there and back in the time it takes the one who is 'he' at hide-and-seek to count to twenty – an age, eyes blind and ears pinned back to follow footfalls on cement or grass and the loose slat in the fence creaking as it tilted; no time for those scrambling to hide, their blood measuring and selling seconds by the yard, hearts' meters ticking over.

Frank joined the girls to watch the first item on *Town and Around*, then Hester called them all up to the table.

Frank waited till only Lex had meat on her plate; she always saved the best for last. He wasn't sure where to begin, then Hester helped him along. She asked Jo, 'Did you go along to Sands' this afternoon?'

Lex hunched over her plate as Jo stored her last mouthful in one cheek and said, 'Thomas was still outdoors. He kept score when we played darts.'

'Do you know,' Frank asked his eldest, 'what will happen to Thomas?'

'Will he die?'

Jo was too abrupt, even for her father, but he rallied. 'He will. Unless his cancer goes into remission. Or someone invents a cure.' The sparsely worded premises of Hamlet's proposition ran in Frank's head: *If it be now, 'tis not to come; if it be not to come, it will be now; if it be not now, yet it will come; the readiness is all.* But the boy's death was beside the point – or – there was *more to it.*

Frank had permitted Jo and Lex to go to Sunday school, because they insisted, because every other kid in the neighbourhood went. Lex had quit when an unChristian Christian classmate waylaid her at the edge of the school field and tore up her colouring-book (the golden calf in three shades of yellow, Moses's wrathful face scarlet crayon under white, blood beneath skin).

'It's always sad when a child dies,' Frank said.

'Partly because it's very rare,' Hester added, watching her daughters' faces for signs of fright. Jo's mouth was prim, her gaze level. She would try to please her father, favour him with her full attention, composed before the sentence of his rationality. Jo knew that to agree with him on these matters – religious matters – meant they were *better* than other people. People with legless arguments about God and Heaven, intoxicated by superstition, who couldn't see straight.

Lex, Hester saw, had wilted when her sister said that Thomas would die, but then, as if watered by the discussion, she unfolded quietly to look up at her father. Steph, sensing a distraction, helped herself to the last potato and gravy and ate quickly while they all talked.

Jo cued her father. 'Glenda says they pray for Thomas.'

'That may help them *feel* better. And, in Thomas's case, as far as I know, his parents have done everything the doctors have recommended. They've tried all treatments known to medical science – radiation therapy and so forth.'

Jo nodded.

'When I was a boy we had neighbours who were Christian Scientists. Their daughter, a pretty girl with blond plaits, was diagnosed as having a brain tumour. Christian Scientists don't believe in modern medicine, only in prayer. The girl's parents wouldn't give the doctors permission to operate on her – not even when she had fits and one eye began to poke out of her head. It was so primitive! They put their faith in God and she died. Her death was terrible, she was young and it was preventable. Their religious beliefs killed her.'

'What's a brain tumour?' Lex asked, horrified by the endless variations of death.

'A cancer that grows in some people's brains. It's *very rare*,' Hester told her.

Frank caught on. He was addressing his remarks mainly to Jo, who had done so well in that Education Department IQ test; but this meat was too gamy for Lex's palate, she was younger, a less robust mind and very impressionable. He said to Lex, 'It won't happen to you.'

Lex couldn't see why not, but chose to trust her father since he obviously knew so much more about death, this villain, this 'man of many guises'. Although brain tumours were patently not in that class of things that could be discounted because they didn't happen *these days* or *in New Zealand* – like the Black Plague or snakebite.

At least Frank stopped short of his litany – how we all, ultimately, go into the ground and rot. Hester wouldn't dispute this, nor was it something that greatly troubled her, but the children shouldn't have to think about it yet. Frank wanted to fortify his children against superstition – and sentimentality. He seemed to object to Christianity as much for what he saw as its sentimentality as for its falsehood.

Hester had tried to explain to him that children are naturally sentimental. They would happily hearken to the sad, come-away strains of *Lassie*. (Frank hated the programme, and the girls kept their mouths shut, secret *Lassie* fans.) Besides, what were the girls supposed to make of going into the ground to rot? Did they even believe it? Earlier that year Jo had written a lovely story about a tram trip to heaven, and given her mother a refreshing glimpse of a glossy twenty-four carat sky through peach blossom clouds. What kind of story would Jo make of going into the ground? Frank was ready with his answers before his daughters had been troubled by the questions. They were wholly, roundly ignorant, without an itch, a suspicion of their deficiencies, souls' shortcomings or bodies' built-in obsolescence.

Frank got up from the table to fetch the brown paper bag of ice-cream cones from the fridge-freezer. He put the bag in the centre of the table and tore it open. The bag exhaled, mist cleared and there were the cones nestled in frost.

Lex found a hole in her ice-cream, an air bubble, sculpturally smooth inside, like a snow cave. She grizzled and was told to 'eat around the hole'. Lex sat and looked at the hole, trying to work out how to move her mouth around an absence. She puzzled, she sulked, finally she burst into tears and her father swapped his cone for hers.

2

It was nine-thirty and Lex had her eyes turned to the window. Current Affairs wound up with a talk about the fight between Cassius Clay and Cleveland 'Big Cat' Williams. Behind the speaker's head Miss Patterson drew down a rolled chart on which was written the eleven-times table. Eleven sevens are seventy-seven. The rhyme of it held Lex's attention for a moment, then she was done with school for the day and wanted, suddenly and acutely, to be at home. She put her hand to the front of her frock and caught hold of the cloth and a small fillet of flesh, twisted her stomach and tried to moan, but couldn't make a sound. That would be to remind everyone of last week's disgrace.

She had had some bug, a gripe in her guts, and had put

up her hand to be excused. She left the room with her friend Avril Arapa, doubled over, her mouth running spit. It was too late. In the toilet she lifted her dress and peered into her pants – they were full of brown faecal mucus. No one offered to help her clean up, instead she was sent home under Avril's escort, walking gingerly with this squelching store of filth between her legs. Her mother hosed her down, dug a hole in the back yard and pursued her panties into it with the hose on hard jet. Then Lex was sent to sit on the toilet till her mother could be sure there was nothing more forthcoming.

Lex knew Avril had told anyone who was interested how she had pooed her pants, and knew they would all stare if she did manage to push a solid sound – a moan – through the hard valve of her mouth. But she wanted to *go*, didn't want to chant the tables, revise her spelling, or stick felt labels by felt figures on a felt backboard, which was supposed to be fun, an *activity* with *equipment*; a shallowly determined world where things and names, colourful and neat – so surely appealing to all little girls – would keep curling up and dropping off.

Lex groaned and everyone looked at her.

'What is it, Lex?'

'It's my stomach.'

Miss Patterson glanced at Avril, who jumped up, her face radiant.

They went together to the toilets, where Lex watched herself in the mirror and tightened her facial muscles in a way that whitened the flesh around her mouth.

Avril took Lex by the arm and led her to the school office. The secretary phoned Hester, who was out. Lex was sent to lie down in the sick-room. Its bed was as bowed as a hammock and the blanket had a label picturing a thistle – and it felt as much. It was quiet in the sick-room, apart from an occasional snore in the long throat of the sink.

Hester and Steph had taken the bus to Lower Hutt. Having only one child at home made Hester feel liberated; that, and this hopping on buses. With Jo she'd stuck to trains and trams and had shopped either at Taita or in town. Jo had motion sickness on motor transport. After the city council began to cut back on trams, even that last stretch to the Zoo, the straight run up Riddiford Street, had Jo white-faced and vomiting. Every trip was an expedition. Hester had carried nappies for the baby and wet cloths to wash Jo's face. Steph was the least obliging of all Hester's children, but she'd sit comfortably on the bus, especially if sweetened by an Eskimo baby or a handful of musky pink smokers. They would go to Woolworths, where Hester could take her time browsing in Haberdashery. If Steph strayed, she could always be found in the toy department parked, covetous, before the toy guns. Hester had already purchased her youngest's Christmas gifts: two six-guns with pearly plastic handles, holsters, a roll of caps, vinyl chaps and waistcoat, a pink ten-gallon hat and tin star.

Latterly, it was only in the school holidays that Hester shopped in town. She would wheel Steph one-handed in her pushchair, and hold Jo's hand. Jo kept hold of Lex, who would stumble across Bowen Street, from the station, her face lifted, staring at the 'man on a horsey', the statue on top of the cenotaph, which she had delighted in since it was first pointed out to her. For once, apparently, it wasn't the horse but the man who thrilled her; his bare torso, straining arm, the yearning supplication that had drawn the marble up under him, like pulled toffee, into a streamlined crag. Poor Hester: a pushchair, one child timid of traffic and another who tripped or dithered, her attention always caught on snags of novelty or drama or sentiment. With her children in tow Hester felt not like an animal with four free limbs but a clump of something complicated, bulky, like tide-borne kelp. Still, town was worth the trouble, the shops were so much more interesting and she could leave the girls to play on the escalators at Wright Stephenson's and rely on them to be there half an hour later. They could lunch at Kirks or meet Frank for a picnic in Bolton Street Cemetery – spread a rug by the Sexton's Cottage where Jo could keep the younger two entertained by collecting gum nuts and 'helicopters' from the sycamore. Town was less practical but more attractive than shopping in the Hutt, or – as Hester called it – 'the great metropolis of Naenae'.

In another six months Steph would be at school and Hester could walk about on her own – step out, swing her arms – except that she couldn't quite remember how to. Her adult life before she had children was with her still, quite clear and whole. She remembered old acquaintances, places, pastimes, herself among it all, but disembodied – she'd lost her memory of all the sensations that would *place* her in her past: of being a different size, smaller; of luxurious late-night wakefulness, a good book and a single bed; of the steel rims of her typewriter keys cupping her fingertips, rings, promissory riches; or the taste of an omelette from Sans Souci, an end-of-the-week lunch treat; and the taste of the cigarette she smoked afterward, the smoke of which had in it somehow the papery flavour of all those neatly typed letters; and the brass of Saturday morning sunlight and Saturday night beer. But this was memory. When Hester became *nostalgic* about being less encumbered it wasn't her single life she remembered, or even the first year of her married life in the mountain guides' quarters at the Hermitage – no, it was her and Frank's flat on Raroa Road. A one-bedroom flat up a flight of wooden steps. Hester had parked Jo's pram under the steps, made it up with sheets and blankets before each trip, and carried both baby and bedding up the stairs every time she came in. They had no washing machine so Hester hand-washed nappies in the bath. The flat was cold and close and steamy, but Jo was good and beautiful, a small baby with fair hair and black eyes. And in the fine weather Hester would get out every afternoon, would wheel Jo along Upland Road and down the Glen, through the Gardens to Tinakori Road and Frank's mother's house. Frank would meet them there and push the pram uphill home. They played 'Whee!', tilting the pram on its two back wheels. 'Whee!' Jo would laugh, her little wallet mouth fat with happiness. Hester's time and tasks were in pieces, but there were moments – like this – when all her feelings and expectations totalled. It wasn't an easy time, but Hester looked back and missed it all – the concentration and intimacy, the good new bread of a first baby, the old trees of central Wellington, days when it rained and she stood with her face to a porthole wiped in the foggy front window, breathless with a loneliness that was like rage.

*

At smoko Mervyn Barrett issued a challenge. They – the *Listener*'s three subs – would each make out a list proposing a number of English language writers who must win the Nobel Prize within the next twenty years.

At five to one Mervyn came back from the pub, where he'd been propping up the bar with a couple of local poets. He had a poem for the editor and gave it to Frank to read in exchange for Frank's list. The other sub, Peter, pushed the door open with his back and came in, re-knotting his knitted tie. Everyone stared. He'd been seen walking in the cemetery with a pretty girl in sandals and op-art earrings – a student maybe. They were reported heading for the place where the trees were thick and the gravestones tilted every which way like boats on choppy water.

Frank flicked the sheet of foolscap. (The poet didn't like stray stanzas on a second page; for longer poems he used longer paper, or he wrote short poems.) 'This is a suicide poem. As a genre it's only slightly above those verses in the *Post*'s In Memoriam column. You know: "We all love our Arthur more, since he flew to a farther shore . . .".'

'It isn't one of his best, but he's a major poet, and it has my vote.'

Frank said, 'You're not doing him any favours you know.'

'He's feeling low. He needs a boost,' Mervyn said, then, 'Christ, Keene! Patrick White?'

'Yes.' Frank put the poem down on Mervyn's desk. 'Boost?' he said. 'Boozed. And it isn't even fit for *The Quaffer's Gazette*.'

'White's absolutely bogus. He overwrites. And he has no ideas – social ideas.'

'Five pounds,' Frank challenged.

Pete passed Mervyn his list. After a moment Mervyn turned to him and asked, 'Durrell?'

'Yes. *The Alexandria Quartet.*'

'Maybe. By the way, what have you two got against Graham Greene? There are a number of very highly praised writers you've both given the go-by.'

'My list is based on my reading, not reputations,' Frank said, rather too haughtily. 'Who says today's taste-makers are backing winners? They could be making the same – same as the famous – mistakes. Like Joyce and Lawrence. And I know what you're going to say,' for Mervyn had drawn himself up. 'That was just prudery, and we are less stuffy.'

'More hip,' Peter said.

'I suspect it's more a matter of time – time for taste to settle – than hipness. Is "ness" the right ending? Or should it be "hipity" like "brevity" and "divinity"?' Frank had begun to wave his arms about. Debating ideas he was never enough at ease to be emphatic without comic exaggeration. Father-less, he was often on the back foot with other men. By which end to pick them up? So he would brood, or play the clown and kidder.

Mervyn was saying something about what Marx, Freud, the death of Queen Victoria and two world wars had done to the twentieth-century mind. He thought it had fewer illusions.

'Of course. We are the great unbenighted generation,' said Frank. 'We know a genius when we see one. We would have backed *The Magic Flute*, and purchased the paintings of Van Gogh.'

'Well, I trust my judgement.' Mervyn put the lists into

an envelope and stowed the envelope in a filing cabinet. 'And after all, these are only opinions.'

Frank sat behind his typewriter and peered at the *something wrong* with his last sentence. 'Shallowly' – worse – 'only shallowly'. He pushed the carriage back and used the X to excise. Often, still, when his good judgement was, to his own mind, proven – in opposition to someone else's poor taste – and pumped up like yeasty dough left to 'prove', then, irritated and scornful and sitting as he was, approximate to a desk, typewriter, blank page, Frank felt he could one day *write that novel*. The one that would conclude with its hero hiding in a cave in the bush. Frank had so much *material*: great, untrammelled nature, the mountains' sudden weather and immense enduring architecture. And his hero, making his way through it all, alone and overawed and speechless – so Frank wouldn't have to 'do' too many people. It felt sound – the solitary character, icy grit, wetas, falling water. It would be good, if he could write it.

But Frank knew that, by the time he was at leisure to sit down and write a novel, *that* novel, planned and nursed, would have dried up – its people and forests desiccated and airy as ash. For in the balance was a savings book for the house in Wadestown, each month's purple ink stamp a fading bruise. And there was his job, last year's fully paid trip to Europe and, every week, his name in print. Besides, Frank had nothing from which to launch himself into the high dive and submerged swim in the surf pool of his own work.

Frank remembered his journals and the fireplace of his bachelor flat in Rolleston Street.

In his search for kindling he took the bath mat of

wooden slats, laid it across the door sill and broke it in two with one foot. You need a good hot fire to burn books, especially books that have travelled on ships, in cabins below the water-line, books full of thick inky definite words, dreams and declarations and covenants with Art. Hester had broken off their engagement. She said he was selfish. He placed the books on the fire, where they lay, for a time not even scorched, the flames sprouting, thin and indolent, like weeds around a paving stone. He put up the fireguard and left the room.

Now, when Frank wound a page into his typewriter to work up his notes or make a record of some odd thing one of the girls had said, he felt as though he had just got off the boat, an immigrant, dispossessed not so much of his language and customs as of orientation – familiar land-marks, steep and shallow grades, rough and smooth places, an old stamping ground. Even if he had the time it would be difficult to begin to write without those past writings; he would set out, but his feet would come down where no step was and he would come a cropper.

Lex woke when Jenny Sand came into the sick-room. The older girl passed her a thermometer. 'The secretary says to put that in your mouth and she'll be in in a tick.' Jenny sat on the floor under the sink. She fiddled with the bloody plug of cotton wool in her left nostril. 'She'll be in in a tick to put a flea in your ear,' she said, then, 'Dad says the Nats are bloated ticks. National,' she explained.

'Jo's interested in all that,' Lex said.

'You're too young.'

'But we're going to watch the election.'

41

'Can you? How?'

'I don't know. Jo says.'

'Hadn't you better put that thing under your tongue? Otherwise it'll read room temperature and they'll decide you're dead.'

Lex tucked the bulb of the thermometer in one cheek.

'I might say you don't look sick.'

'That's because you're used to looking at your brother.'

'I suppose so.' Jenny pulled out the bloody plug, inspected it, snuffled experimentally and quickly replaced it. 'But we didn't realise Thomas was sick for ages. Till the day Mum saw him coming home up the right-of-way, and he was dragging his feet, like he was exhausted. Then when he was in the tub she noticed all these bruises on his legs. He said Glenda had kicked him – she had, but not hard enough to bruise like that. Mum and Dad took him to the Doctor and we found out how sick he was.'

'Didn't he know?' Lex asked around the thermometer.

'He was used to it.'

That anyone could be sick like that and not know. Lex shifted the glass stick, swizzling her spit; it pressed against the hinge of her tongue. She knew that to take a pulse meant counting the small flicks in her wrist but didn't know what amounted to good health. Sometimes her heartbeat troubled her, echoing out of her pillow. But to sicken, to die, seemed something the whole world was more apt to do, in dull weather or at the day's end when it cooled away from a girl, from her eyes and ears and skin.

Jenny said, thoughtfully, 'Jo must mean to hang around a polling booth. Funny girl.'

Lex tried to figure this out, but only came up with the

42

title of a book Jo had read: *The Phantom Tollbooth*. It sounded even more frightening than standing under the rail bridge when the trains went over. Hayley wouldn't want to come.

'You're all funny girls,' Jenny said.

Lex didn't like to be baffled. Particularly when she needed to know she was well and would live. The mercury in the glass wand had stopped at the red line, which seemed good, but Lex could feel her blood only temporarily coherent, like a trail of ants. The lunch bell rang and Lex got off the bed. She thrust the thermometer at Jenny and bolted from the room.

Lunch monitors, big kids, would see if she broke cover and ran for the end of the field – out-of-bounds – the long grass under the birches and the stand of fennel. Every child in the school sat on forms outside the classrooms to eat lunch and swing their legs. Lex hid under the hydrangea bush beside the incinerator. And collected herself. Gathered in –

The lights of Mount Victoria from the deck of an overnight ferry. Daddy buttoned her into his overcoat. He said words and warm nonsense: Lex. Look. Cold. Snuggle down, Lex. At Christchurch the girl cousin had a Wendy house. She was daddy, Jo was mummy, but Lex didn't want to be baby. Lex was a big girl, one and a half. The boy cousin chased Lex with his mother's shears, then threatened to sever his mother's stuffed draught-stopper. Sausage dog. Puffing Billy. The black engine they were taken to see.

And, earlier yet, Lex could remember her playpen: the smeary bars, the sun, a sward – lawn – a horizon of vegies; Daddy, digging, framed in the frill of her bonnet. Jo came to the bars and shook Poochy-pup. The warm swooned and

43

the lawn frowned. Poochy cocked his knitted ears at the cloud. Lex made Jo show her back and undone sash by throwing Poochy over the top rail of the playpen. Mummy came down the back steps with boiled water for the ants' nest. She stooped and poured; Lex smelled steamed dust, formic acid, the mint by the drain.

Lex brushed chaff out of a hollow in the hard-packed earth. The hydrangeas had grown over an old marbles patch. Marbles were banned – the commerce of swapsies had led to theft, it was said. Teachers hated fads; fads organised the children, and fired them up far too much. After all, schools are models of society – mass movements and fervour are only sanctioned when they come down from above.

Lex got up and shook the leaf-litter from her dress. She felt not so much soothed as hungry. Her ability to concentrate wasn't equal to the dread she felt considering Thomas's illness. Like a bubble trapped under her hand in the bath Lex's attention would wander, buoyant and ticklish, then float free, lose its boundaries and melt into the general air. She had forgotten her heartbeat and remembered the brown paper bag in her desk – sandwiches, an apple, Sun Maid raisins, and Hayley's shop-bought custard square that was always a little too much for one.

After school Jo explained the universe to Hayley and Lex. Jo stood at the bathroom sink cleaning a skeleton, all that remained of the corpse of a bird she and Lex had spoken rites over some months before. The younger girls sat on the edge of the bath while Jo soaped the bones and scrubbed them with her toothbrush. Steph came in to tell them

Lampchop was on, but was arrested by Jo's inventory.

'We live on a planet in orbit around the sun, in the Solar System – which means us and all the other planets. Then there are other suns – all the stars are suns – which make up the galaxy, the Milky Way. Then there are other galaxies, thousands, which make up the universe. So the universe is bigger than – ' Jo, boggled, stretched out both her arms, her toothbrush dripping brown and white foam onto the bathroom lino. 'Bigger than the whole world.' She stamped her foot. 'Damn!' Damn the primers and their illustrated 'big' list: house, tree, car, elephant, bulldozer.

Lex wanted to know was the universe the same as out-of-space?

'*Outer* space. Yes. Except the universe means here too.'

Hayley asked, 'Here?' And Jo told her about the globe they had in Room Five, how they had 'looked up' New Zealand, how much better a globe was than a map for seeing how the land lay.

Steph wanted to know what New Zealand was.

Hayley was proud to explain. 'Here. The country we live in.'

Steph asked, aggrieved, 'Don't we live in America?'

The others laughed.

Lex wanted to know if the universe included made-up places, like Bedrock, Sherwood Forest, Heaven and the Wild West.

'Only everywhere real,' Jo said, and that the Wild West *was* real. She rinsed her toothbrush, put it back in the rack and placed the gleaming, foamy handful of bones on the windowsill. Then she began to list the nine planets.

But Steph had gone off to see Fergie Fang, Hayley was reaching for the bird skull, and Lex was saying, '*Was* is real,' not like someone starting an argument but like a smaller child playing a private game.

'Hayley! Put that down! Let's go watch *Shari Lewis*. Hurry, last weeks!' Jo said, like the cinema ads. She herded the girls out of the bathroom.

After *Travellers' Tales*, Lex walked Hayley back home then went up onto the stopbank to see if she could spot the big boys' fort. Among the willows she saw raised dust, and heard the sound of a sheet of tin shaken. It was warmer today and seed-pods popped in the last of the sunlight, a sound like someone stirring on a woven cane chair. As Lex walked along the top of the stopbank the sun was snuffed out by the hills above the river, its rays swept upward then flattened into feverish whiteness over half the sky. The scrub ticked like a cooling engine. Then Lex could hear wind in gorse prickles and the boys talking about mines and booby-traps.

Some day soon Lex would keep a watch for the boys to leave, count them all out, then go and see. For Lex feats of engineering were about the creation of new perspectives. She had wondered about the view from excavations, bridges, tall buildings, ever since the day she and Jo had ventured into a drainpipe.

Its outfall was the river bank, where the two girls stood on a welcome mat of smooth silt and looked at the perfect black circle of the drain mouth. Jo climbed inside. It was dry, she reported, and there were a few stones at the bottom, but it wasn't too close or uncomfortable. *Come in Lex.* They crawled a short way. The curve of the pipe bent Lex's hands at painful angles, grit chafed her palms. It was cold, and a cold hush pushed at her eardrums. Jo had to bargain with Lex to make her go on. 'If you follow me you can smack my bottom.' For a younger sister this was a privilege not to be turned down. They went on with giggles and thwacks. 'Ouch, ouch,' Jo said, her voice a sonar echo.

They crawled seventy feet and came out in a culvert beneath Taita Drive. Light shone through the bars of a drain on wet green walls and – in a few inches of water – a comb, a rusted bolt, a pearly bottle and plastic rain hat. The girls could hear traffic and children playing: the tinkle and slap of a musical skipping rope; shouts, and deep-voiced sobbing from David Hough, the boy in callipers whom everyone teased. It sounded different, distinct – the girls listened more attentively – and innocent, or uninformed, because the skipper, shouter, sobber, were being overheard from an unguessable place.

On the return trip Lex was afraid. The novelty had worn off smacking Jo, and besides, Jo was in her way – the mouth of the drain appeared as a tiny white sun over Jo's back, then afterward a broken circle past her sister's slow, obstructive body.

Lex scrambled back down the home side of the stopbank. It was tea time and the street was quiet. The Keenes ate closer to – as Frank complained – society hours, so Lex knew she wasn't yet missed. As she passed Sands' she heard her name called and looked about. A window was open into the narrow gap between the side of the house and the neighbours' fence. Thomas was hooking his hand at her.

She came on to the edge of the property then was barred by a low hedge.

'Push through it,' Thomas whispered.

The hedge grazed her legs, but she was quick and it scarcely stung. She stopped beneath his window and put her hand on the wall where the weatherboards were still warm from a glancing sun.

Thomas folded his arms on the sill. In this light his skin looked dark, congested with the colour behind him – not a dim room but the unlined purple curtains. 'I've been sent to bed; not for being bad but "too seedy", Dad says. What do you think of that?'

'Seedy is short for going to seed,' Lex said. This was what passed for an opinion with her. 'Are you in bed?'

'My feet are.'

Lex could recall being sent to bed, in the afternoon, sick with the English measles, and how she woke at evening to a borderline light and the curtains open. 'Once when I was sick in bed I woke up – ' Lex began, the recollection flat against her face like cold glass. 'The sun was going like – ' she ran her hand along the weatherboards, ' – *now*. It was the same window in our house. This window on this side.' Their houses were identical, but that the Keenes' was asbestos clad. 'The edges of the window were all yellow and the sky was blue. So blue – '

'Because you were shut in when everyone else had gone down to the river for a swim.' Thomas tried to help her out, this younger child who, as she spoke, blew up in his face, as gradual and fierce as a Mount Vesuvius, Fairy Rain, or Flower Pot.

'No, not fine, blue. Blue you can't breathe. Like, suppose

48

there wasn't any air on the other side of the window. Or not much. Like on top of mountains. Like Sir Edmund Hillary and the oxygen tanks.'

'I've had oxygen.'

'Isn't it just another word for air?'

'No. It's special rich air.'

'Is it nice?'

'Yes.' Thomas seemed tired, he laid his head on his arms.

Lex looked at him with her mouth open – trying to imagine the different taste of oxygen to air, like cream to milk, then she went on: 'Suppose you are on top of a high mountain, without oxygen tanks – ' She made a swift search of her father's mountain stories and found, ' – the summit. You're on the summit and it's like a desert island. The air below you is the sea, the air above is the sky, freezing cold but not frozen and all blue. That was my blue.'

Thomas simply looked at her, quiet, his eyes cleared of colour by the dusk and curiously doll-like between their unfringed lids. Then he asked, with effort, 'Was it real?'

'I don't know.'

'Were you scared?'

'Not that something would happen, but I shut my eyes.'

Thomas moved his head to look along the gap between the house and the neighbours' fence. At, perhaps, some kin of Lex Keene's blue. The spindly hawthorn, each branch, twig, spine and blossom black against the sky, looked like the template of all flowering trees. There again was the other world that seemed, often now, to pull up and park beside his own.

Thomas felt four icy pressure points on his forehead and when he opened his eyes – they had been closed – he saw the palm of Lex's hand, a shallow rosy cave. She drew back. 'You went to sleep,' she said.

Pain ran a comb through Thomas's bones and he came apart, slid back without a word onto his bed leaving the window unlatched. Lex called his name and listened. Silence made an emphatic reply. The room's darkness seemed organic, and the furry mildew that dotted the windowsill like spores dropped of that darkness.

Frank caught his train well before the six o'clock swill. But it was still packed. He hefted his satchel into the luggage rack – already bulging, an overstuffed string bag – and stood holding on to a chrome knob on the end of a seat. The doors shut, the unit chirruped and set out from the shelter of platform five. The commuters flipped up the corners of their newspapers or narrowed their eyes against the glare from the platform of polished patches of old chewing gum, then the dazzle of broken glass between browned stones.

Frank stood facing a newspaper ad, a picture of Holyoake rising above a ripped-out headline: Britain's New Moves to Enter European Common Market. The slogan read: More Than Ever Leadership Counts. Frank inaudibly advised leadership not to count its chickens but its days, then looked around for something better to read.

It was near dark when Frank got off the train. And when he turned the corner where Taita Drive curved to follow the river there was more light from the street lamps than the sky – and from kitchens, domestic yellow electricity. The houses hadn't yet drawn their blinds, so Frank could see into every kitchen (at the front left corner of every house, repetitiously, kids at kitchen tables, mothers at sinks). State houses, the street like a strip of film spooling between the shops at Pomare and those at Taita.

Frank saw Lex in her school clothes and pinafore coverall. She ran towards him – all sprint, no skip – as if in fright. But she hadn't seen him and he watched her turn down the path to the house and pause, as he planned to, to look for people in their kitchen.

'Less', she had called herself when she was younger and lisping still. Less. No parent is as intimate with a second child as a first. Frank had no notebooks of Lex's odd, childish remarks, or folders of scribbles. He had misfiled the curl from her first haircut, and his camera had broken shortly before her second birthday and hadn't been replaced. Jo was odd and, as the IQ test confirmed, highly intelligent. It was Jo he played pieces of music and lectured on the composers' lives. Jo he read bits of Tolstoy and Proust. He hoped Jo would grow up able to appreciate the achievements of great men. He hoped she'd be a like mind – perhaps write him letters about concerts or museum visits from the great cities of the world.

But Lex – Lex was born by emergency caesarean. Hester was white and depleted and weaned the baby at six weeks. Lex was colicky and, while Hester slept, Frank would walk the baby – curled up around her gripe and crying in long, exhausted screams – walk her up and down the kitchen. Since then she would always at least pause to reassess her distress if he asked her, 'Don't cry, Curly.' It made him feel able, and he loved her. He had no plans for his second daughter but her happiness.

Frank's daughters were in the lounge, sitting in the cool animated light of the television. This was a recent shift in the polarity of half the houses in the street. At evening previously unused front rooms – polished pianos and wedding photos or, in the Keenes' case, the bookcases and radiogram in its oak cabinet – were now full of kitchen chairs, still children and the demons of these broached Pandora's boxes: *The Adventures of Rin Tin Tin, Travellers' Tales, Cameras on the Campus.*

Frank remembered standing hand-in-hand with Lex on the footpath outside a neighbour's house, at dusk, watching through a window the first television on the street. There was something wrong with the vertical hold and the image scrolled up and up. He had to explain to Lex that this wasn't how TV told its stories – like those toy televisions in vogue with children; made with a box, two sticks, and a roll of paper on which pictures were drawn – a scroll of comic panels (Lex: 'And then the children find a Martian hiding in a tree . . .').

Steph was picking her nose. Frank tapped on the window and all three girls started, then laughed.

3

The book Glenda had chosen for the week was about dreams. It was bedtime and Thomas was in bed, and dreamy. The people in the book – Marianne and Mark – their tiredness was catching. Thomas made to yawn, tried to gulp down sleepiness. But he was tired rather than sleepy – and frying in discomfort, hot, curling up at the edges.

'And sure enough,' Glenda read, and her voice waned like a radio slipping off the station, 'she had hardly lain down for the night before she was asleep, and asleep was dreaming.'

Glenda had once saved a life; Thomas was there and saw it. The previous summer, on perhaps his last long walk –

he was tired then, but undiagnosed – Thomas had trailed along the river bank after Glenda and her boyfriend. The teenagers picked a spot by the rail bridge where the river was too swift for swimming, away from all the other picnickers, locals, the kids adrift on patched inner tubes. Glenda and her boyfriend laid their towels among the boulders, edge to edge on a mat of gravel. Glenda unfastened the back strap of her bikini and held its stiffened cups carefully against her breasts as she lay down. Her boyfriend smoothed Coppertone onto her back. 'Go away, droopy,' Glenda said to her brother, 'but not near the water.'

Thomas went the other way, clambered over progressively larger boulders, deposited by remote floods in the years before the city began to milk the Hutt's white headwaters. Under the rail bridge Thomas found Jo and Lex Keene, and Hayley Moynihan. They stood by the first cement pile, on a shelf hacked from the river bank. There was enough room for a tall man to stand upright, his head touching the steel girders of the bridge, or for children ten and under to stand on tiptoe reaching, without being able to touch. The shelf was completely dry and littered with broken glass (brown beer bottles) and charred wood from campfires. The bridge piles themselves were sticky and stank of urine.

The girls were waiting for a train, for the clamour of a train passing at speed above their heads. They had been swimming and were still damp, wet cotton togs gathered to their bodies by row after row of shirring elastic. They were grubby, uncomfortable, expectant.

The wind shifted and the children were warned by a gust of noise, the bells at the crossing on Taita Drive. The rails sizzled. Hayley began to shout; she covered her ears. The ground trembled. The noise bore down on them, full spate, and swept everything away. They yelled, Thomas too, and danced in terror, in exaltation.

Then it had passed; the bridge shivered into solidity and only the rails telegraphed back the sound of wheels dropping across each join – clank-clank, clank-clank – a quarter, then a half mile up the line.

'Let's wait for the next one,' Thomas said.

'Clickity-click, clickity-click,' Hayley chanted, 'sixty-six, clickity-click!'

Lex picked up a charred stick and began to draw on the pile – a cupboard and crockery; a rack with dangling kitchen forks, spoons, fish slice, potato masher; then, against the right angle of earth, a cat of snowman simplicity, two circles, ears, tail, whiskers.

Hayley had another blackened stick and was drawing, blasphemously, holes in her own hands while singing the peanut song:

> A peanut sat on the railroad track
> his heart was all a-flutter
> along came a train, the nine-fifteen
> toot toot, peanut butter!

As they waited someone walked by, overhead, limped from tie to tie – all the children recognised the wheezing hinge of David Hough's callipers. A minute after David passed the rails sizzled again, and Thomas's and Jo's eyes met, alarmed. They ran out from under the bridge to see that – No! – David was only halfway across and had come to a halt looking up the line. He turned and began a hopping run back the way he'd come.

The children could see the train, a rattler, carriages drawn by a diesel engine – a big blunt front with a cow-catcher ploughing the air before it. Thomas and Jo began to shout encouragement to the limping boy. The train gave a blast of its horn, a megaphonic groan. Hayley stood gaping. The train horn sounded again, then the train began to brake. Lex ran back under the bridge and pressed her face into her imaginary kitchen cabinet; charcoal smeared her forehead and cheeks.

The train was on the bridge. David looked back over his shoulder and lunged forward, his shirt-tail flapped and the brace on his leg flashed in the sun. Then Thomas saw Glenda and her boyfriend stand up from among the boulders. The boyfriend put his hands to his head and pressed his skull; his eyes seemed to move farther apart, as if he was searching for an aperture through which an idea might make its way. Glenda had forgotten to hold herself together and Thomas stared at his sister's breasts. His eyes, in expectation of blood and violence, had never seen anything so tender and lovely. Glenda waved her arms and shrieked, 'Hang over the side!' She yelled this over and over, till David Hough, the train nearly upon him, veered to the edge of the bridge, caught hold of a protruding tie and dropped. The train crossed the place he had stood. He swung, shuddering with the bridge.

The train slowed to a stop, half of one carriage still on the bridge. The driver climbed out onto the footplate of the engine and looked back along the track. Glenda's boyfriend had scrambled up the embankment and onto the bridge to haul David to his feet. The driver began to shout, something about the police, prosecution. Glenda sat down on a rock and fastened her bikini; shook herself into it. The driver had a radio telephone – he shouted – that cretin had better stay put, the police would want to speak to him. Commuters had pushed their windows up and were peering out. 'You see to it!' the driver bawled. Glenda's boyfriend waved. David Hough sobbed and gasped, there were candlesticks of snot on his top lip and Glenda's boyfriend held him by the shirt – had done touching him for the moment.

'He'll get the belt, I bet,' Hayley said.

'Perhaps he'll be fined or sent to prison,' Thomas said.

'Borstal. Boys go to borstal.' Jo knew these things.

'His daddy will give him a good hiding.' Hayley relished the idea.

Thomas looked around. 'Where's Lex?'

Lex crouched halfway up the stopbank wiping her hands back and forth across the grass. Her hands were grey, reeking, and there was a streak of oil on her face, blacker than the charcoal. 'It came from the train,' she explained. 'It dripped down on me. I thought it was his blood.'

Glenda sat at the end of Thomas's bed. As she read she squeezed his foot through the covers – the counterpane. *Peter Pan*. She said he should try to put his pain into his shadow. But his shadow was a patch of mist, a warm breath shrinking on a cold windowpane. Was he confused? Hadn't they finished *Peter Pan* last week? Tonight it was *Marianne Dreams*. The book was face down on the bedspread. Glenda was at the door, calling, 'Mum! He's bad!'

This time the pain followed as the fever let go and left him settling slowly into a boy-shaped print of sweat, his pyjamas wet beneath him. He was like a piece of toast not put into a rack to cool but laid flat, left softening in its own steam. The fever relented but the pain followed, feeding still.

He wept – dry, weak, persistent – then slept for a short while. There was no gloss left in his young skin and his eyelids looked loose, crepey. The usual marvellous variations in colouring – blush, freckle, subterranean blues of venous blood – he had none of it, nothing but liverish yellow, contusions and pallor.

Thomas's mother folded the sheet back firmly, away from his face. He whined. If she could manage tonight, she thought. Only. If only she could manage only tonight –

The year had gone down in manageable pieces, and she had kept it down, days, nights, hospital visits. It was not an ordeal, it was – only – a dish she had not calculated was so burning hot, a dish containing tonight's dinner that she must not drop till she reached the bench. Not an ordeal – just one of her babies at three a.m. *Just necessary.*

Thomas's mother saw him to the lavatory in the early hours of the morning. When he had finished he wouldn't wipe himself, couldn't get up again. He slumped against the wall with his head hung. When she tried to move him he cried out – a piteous, angry, mindless complaint – as if he didn't know she meant the best for him; or didn't know her at all.

4

On the morning of Election Saturday Jo, Lex and Hayley took up a post on top of the cement milk-box at the gate to Pomare School. A sign stood on the path: *Polling Booth*. It had rained overnight and there were puddles on the asphalt, some filmed with oil and synthetically bright rainbows. The sun had been out for some time and the air was redolent of steam, solvents, car fumes.

The girls told everyone who came in at the gate to please vote Labour. Most laughed, a few frowned, one man asked them had their parents put them up to it. After half an hour Jo's Mr Heron appeared and gave each girl sixpence to take to the dairy and buy an ice-cream.

They strolled home licking their lime or tutti-frutti or

orange and chocolate-chip triple scoops, and Jo advised Hayley to work her tongue around the ice-cream to prevent dribbles of melt softening its cone. A wind got up and Hayley's hair dabbled in the ice-cream. 'Yum,' she said, 'I like elections.'

Hester and Frank sat at the kitchen table looking over the architect's drawings of the Mairangi Road house, those and a bundle of papers: specifications, permits and builders' quotes.

'It has to be right if I'll be paying for it the rest of my life.'

The floor plan had pictographs: parallel bars for stairs; a small circle for the toilet; larger quarter circles to show where doors were hinged, which way they swung. Hester read 'window', 'ranch-slider', 'deck', 'basement', 'built-in shelving'. The frontage was 'north facing'. All the names, figures, symbols seemed charms to Hester. She would get up into the gallery above Churchill Drive and Wilton's Bush. It might not be the city's gallery, or a country seat, but it was still several degrees above the cheap seats of the Hutt Valley.

Hester had enjoyed her Pomare neighbours, although it had taken her some time to realise how different their lives and expectations were from her own. The differences surprised her, and she was surprised at herself for not anticipating such differences – not deficits, just departures.

Take the Robbs, who had lived next door when Lex was a baby. Each spring several litters of kittens got a start in life under the Robbs' house, and scrapped among the Robb girls' dismembered dolls, the boys' dismantled trucks and bits of a broken vacuum-cleaner Mrs Robb had bought – hire purchase – then let one son use to clean his bantams' cage. Hester's mother, up from Christchurch on a badly timed visit – Jo and Lex had mumps, followed almost immediately by chickenpox – said to Hester, one afternoon when the Robb children were charging up and down outside on bikes while Hester's spotty daughters soaked in a bath full of baking soda, that perhaps *her* girls would do better on Coca-Cola and chips like *that lot*.

Mrs Robb was a romancer. She would stand at the fence while Hester pegged out nappies telling Hester how the family's corgi was related to the Queen's; or how her Rolly was a war hero, unrecognised through some administrative oversight; or how scared she was for her youngest – a little girl in flounced nylon frocks whose top lip was frequently varnished with snot. Wendy was delicate, she said, and had been given extreme unction *twice* now.

This was all very diverting for Hester. She was mystified by the numerous salesmen who knocked at the Robbs' but always gave the Keenes the go-by. Then the Robbs moved, quite suddenly it seemed, and when Hester rang State Advances about a cat her neighbours had left behind, it turned out that State Advances had no idea their tenants had gone, or where they had got to. 'They did a flit,' another neighbour said, and laughed at Hester's account of the salesmen. 'Those were debt collectors.'

That neighbouring house, like their own, was a pool house for state servants. The Moynihans down the road lived in a Railways house; Pat Moynihan was a guard on the units. His wife, Queenie, kept every room dark, to stop the furnishings from fading – even the blinds in the kitchen were half-mast. Queenie sat in an umber twilight listening to 2ZB, Doreen dispensing advice. The radio somehow made her kitchen cheerful, even with the fine weather shut out; those callers, their rising inflections, the ease of Doreen.

The Keenes' other next-door neighbours had different surnames – Hester realised after having known them over a year. They were in a de facto marriage. 'Same as,' the neighbour said, 'half the street.' The neighbour was tolerant of Hester's raised brows, and her awkward attempt to back pedal. 'It hadn't even crossed my mind that you weren't – um.'

Hester had enjoyed the Hutt's different peoples, but not the valley's short winter days, the lawn that seldom dried, was filmed with water or smooth silt beads of worm-castings, that grew birds rather than daisies, so that her daughters learned as toddlers more than the generic 'bird' and could identify starling, sparrow, thrush, blackbird and, most discouraging, the gulls that mobbed sulkily on the stopbank in certain kinds of bad weather. Hester hated having to take in her washing at three in midwinter, when the sun went behind the hills; hated the flat, barren walks; the old bombs on front lawns and the more vulgar fads the children lent themselves to – like chewing tar picked off the road.

Hester left Frank in charge of lunch and went out to vote. When his older daughters didn't appear Frank called Steph in from the back yard. Her sleeves and trouser legs were wet. 'I've been riding my tricycle all morning,' she said. He sat her at the table and made her luncheon-sausage sandwiches, then taught her to take alternate bites of spring onion. She didn't talk but seemed happy to have him to herself.

Jo and Lex turned up at the same time as their mother. Hester looked troubled. Rumours of a disappointing result? But, of course, it was hours till the polls closed, Frank told himself.

Jo and Lex had been given lunch at Moynihans'. 'Because we helped pick the raspberries,' said Jo.

'We ate at a tray table in the garden. Saveloys and sandwich bread,' said Lex. 'And cordial. Pineapple, not lemon and barley-water.'

Jo relayed a message. 'Mr Moynie says you should come over later for a beer. Everyone else is. I've picked some fresh duckweed.' She went out to her tadpoles.

'Hayley taught me to play "Can you wash your Daddy's shirts" on the piano,' Lex said. 'And Mr Moynie's going to kill one of the chooks.'

Steph piped up. 'Mummy, I've been a good girl. I ate an onion.'

Hester sat down, still wearing her coat. Frank watched her as he filled the percolator, put fresh grounds in the basket and put the pot on. (This partiality to real coffee, rather than tea, or instant, was – in their neighbours' eyes – the Keenes' greatest oddity.) The hot plate creaked as it warmed, and the coffee pot souffled like a man calling a cat.

Jo ran back inside, in tears. Big John and Mayflower were dead, floating belly-up. Little John had keeled over and was swimming in circles. The bucket was only half full.

They all went outside to see. Frank carefully removed

the river stones and duckweed then squatted back on his heels waiting to speak to Jo. She continued to cry, hard.

'Do you think a dog got in and drank the water?' Lex asked.

Steph said, 'Maybe they fainted.'

No one responded.

'Little John doesn't have much life left in him, Snowy,' Frank said. 'You don't want him to suffer, do you?'

Jo shook her head.

Hester put out a foot and pressed it into the ground beside the bucket. Squelch.

'I should put him out of his misery,' Frank said.

Jo nodded; she felt that she was upsetting someone other than her parents, who didn't like to see her cry. Maybe Little John, who would perhaps prefer to be put out of *her* misery.

Lex watched the bands of sunlit water on the walls of the green bucket, and three shadows, two flotsam, one still under its own propulsion.

'Come inside and wash your face, pet,' Hester said. 'Wash your face and you'll feel better.' She took Jo's hand and led her in.

'What will you do with him?' Lex asked her father.

'While Jo's in the bathroom I'll pour them down the stormwater drain.'

'Maybe he'll get better,' Lex said. She imagined Little John making his way out of the drainpipe, as she had, to the outfall on the river bank, then somehow from the outfall to the river – no place for frogs, but she wasn't to know that.

'Maybe he will,' her father agreed.

*

Their mother had dressed her mouth with lipstick. She asked the girls whether they would all come along the road.

'I suppose so.' Jo stood, knock-kneed, her whole body unhappy and tending inward.

Jo's mother didn't remark on this; she was pulling at her own fingers as though adjusting a pair of gloves. 'Girls?'

Steph looked up, but Lex had just reached the part where Grendel 'rends' the men 'limb from limb to drink the warm blood'.

'Lex?'

'What!'

'Mind your tone, pet.'

Lex closed her book.

'Did you finish that book of puzzles Grandma gave you?'

'No. Only the connect-the-dots.'

Hester pulled up a chair and sat. She said, 'Thomas went to hospital last night. I met his daddy at the polling booth. I said I'd visit him tomorrow.'

The girls waited.

'And I thought it would be nice to take him some things to keep him busy if he has to stay there.'

Jo asked, 'Is that what they expect, that he'll be in hospital for a while?' Here was an opportunity to demonstrate a virtue – generosity. If only she could think of something she could bear to part with.

'I don't know where that book of puzzles is now,' Lex said.

'I've already found it. And I thought you might like to give him the space capsules you've been collecting.'

There were 'stages' of Gemini and Saturn rockets in

Puffed Wheat packets. It seemed to take more breakfasts than three girls could get through to assemble a whole rocket. But they had four capsules already, so could practise splash-downs.

'No! Not those!' Jo protested.

'But you scarcely ever play with them, Jo.'

'Because they aren't *finished*.'

Hester lost her temper. 'How can you be so selfish! What selfish girls.'

Jo burst into tears. 'Let him have something else.'

Hester got up. 'Forget I even mentioned it.' For the next several minutes she banged about the kitchen, wrapping a batch of coconut roughs for Queenie. Then she stood at the sink, sighing through her nose.

Jo left the kitchen then returned with the rocket stages in her cupped hands – white plastic cones and cylinders stamped with red lettering, 'USA', and a stripe of chequered red and white. Jo deposited her offering by Hester's handbag. Lex looked at the pile sadly. There went most of the props for the space-race game. The Russians would win by default – the Russians flew cardboard cigar tubes.

'Thank you, Jo.' Hester put the parcel of biscuits under her arm and called Frank who was in the lounge listening to Mahler – the one Jo called 'Earwig, earwig' – *The Song of the Earth*. 'Just sing out when you're ready,' he had said.

Frank fetched two bottles of beer he'd had cooling in the fridge door and they all went over to Moynies'.

All the windows of the corner kitchen were open, there were beer glasses on the sills, and elbows, rolled sleeves and brown arms. Pat Moynie had just mown the front lawn;

he hadn't a grass catcher so the lawn was thick with mulch, and the children were green of joint. Hayley's brothers were playing swing-ball – thwack – the whippy rod quivered as the shuttle-puppy reversed its orbit. Inside, Lex and Hayley twisted to 'Do the Bluebeat': 'A-chicky-chick, a-chicky-chicky-chang-chang . . .' Laddie the collie pulled down the clothes prop and Queenie's washing lay muddled like bunting the day after some public celebration. Naomi Arapa looped the end of her elastics around the Moynies' letter-box. Jo stood in the other end while Naomi set out to master thighsies. Her parents were indoors being teased about the votes they'd wasted on Social Credit. Queenie moistened the chook she was slowly roasting, wrapped in layers of damp newsprint. The eldest Arapa boy drove his bomb up and down the road with children standing on its running boards. Mr Moynie moved the dial to listen to the news.

Lex put her hand on the shed door, the milled grip of its round handle. She looked back. Her family were in the lounge watching an election special that had interrupted her programmes: *Thunderbirds*, *Mighty Atom*, *The Adventures of Robinson Crusoe*.

Honeysuckle grew about the door like kiss curls around a face. The sheet-asbestos of the shed walls still radiated warmth, and the flowers warm fragrance.

Lex's father stored empty beer bottles on narrow shelves formed by the shed's frame. They stood in rows up against the black builder's paper that lined the shed. Two new bottles were by the door, the only two still free of dust.

Lex liked beer and enjoyed draining dregs from the stored bottles, never mind that it was flat or warm – it reminded her of fresher swallows she might beg from Daddy's glass.

Lex tilted the first bottle. The beer was thicker than water – bitter spit. In the next bottle something rustled, but it was too late, Lex's lips already sealed the glass neck. Something tumbled into her mouth with the liquid, something resilient and living. It stung her tongue. She spat out onto the cement floor, a wasp, alive, sorting itself out from her spit and the sugary beer that was its temptation.

Her mouth was an agony in which she had no separate sensations of teeth, tongue, gums – it was all one pain. Lex stepped on the wasp, ground her foot, husked it of its hard skeleton. It was revenge and automatic; then, with more presence of mind, she stowed the bottle back on its shelf.

She hunkered down by the outside tap, held her tongue under its stream. The water cooled the hurt, but left a halfpenny-sized patch in the centre of her tongue that was completely numb. Numb, like a scab, to everything but pressure.

Inside Lex found her mother spooning peas from a colander onto five plates.

'I'm not hungry,' Lex said, achieving a perfect French 'r' in the back of her throat.

To Hester it sounded like babyish English. 'It's mock-chicken, Lex.'

Lex liked mock-chicken, salty ground meat, shaped like a drumstick and nicely caramelised at its thin end against the meat-skewer bone. But, tender of her mouth, she shook her head.

'No?' Hester said. She came and laid a palm against Lex's forehead, then the back of her hand as a second

68

opinion. Lex was her usual pale olive shade, and ripe of eye.

'I can't eat because,' Lex began – and her thought flew, not towards the blurred green beyond the dartboard, or a wire at best, but towards the open-pored, painted cork of the dartboard proper, a bull's-eye – 'because Thomas is sick.'

'Oh, Lex,' her mother said, exasperated, but touched too.

'Really,' Lex said.

'I can't force you to eat. You go tell the others their tea is on the table.'

Lex fetched them all, then sat herself on the kitchen floor so that the food was out of her line of sight. Her father was telling Jo that the music to *The Adventures of Robinson Crusoe* was 'The Moldau' by Smetana. He promised to play it later. He and Jo were unusually quiet throughout the meal. Jo was mourning her tadpoles, and her father the election.

'General mourning,' he said to Hester.

'It's not yet absolutely certain.'

'What's *wrong* with this country?'

'They prefer strict parents.'

Frank smiled at his wife, then asked, 'Why isn't Lex eating?'

'She's upset about Thomas.'

'You should still eat, Curly.'

'I can't.'

'Don't lisp, pet. You're a big girl,' Hester reminded her.

'I told you she's the empathic one,' Frank said. He turned to Lex. 'Why don't you write Thomas a letter? Mummy can take it to him tomorrow when she visits. Or you could draw him a picture.' When Frank was in England at the end of '65 he had loved Lex's letters: 'Dear Daddy. I are on a Journal now. Grandmar has got the phone on now. Aunty Paulie is staying with us. Mummy bought some blue and white material for me. Paulie has cut my hair. Steph has her hair in a ribbon. Paulie cut Jo hair to. I have got a book from the library its name is how to oose. Are you good Daddy? Love from Lex.'

Frank said, 'Come sit up at the table. I'll get you some paper. Perhaps once you've written to Thomas you might feel more like tea?'

Lex sat at the table and swallowed the spit that had pooled under her tongue. Her father gave her some paper – not the usual waste-paper from his office with programme listings printed on one side, but a fresh sheet. Lex saw she would have to apply herself, at least till the gravy jelled in the dish where her mock-chicken drumsticks lay in reserve. She doubted her excuse could stand reheating.

She drew a car and tow-truck; as a boy Thomas would like that. Then she forgot her audience and remembered only letters – so wrote, 'Dear Thomas, I hope you are well . . .'

5

Sunday, and Lex was at a loose end. Jo, still in mourning, had kept home to finish writing her book, *Honey and John on Windy Hill.* Jo planned to send it to Thomas on her mother's next visit – or take it to him herself; she liked the notion of a hospital visit.

The whole street was quiet, as if convalescing. Although it was a fine, still day very few adults were out-of-doors.

Lex spent her morning over the stopbank, by herself in her grotto – as Jo called it – a cavern formed by convolvulus which grew to cover the branches of a dead willow. The grotto was special to Lex because she had claimed the old sewing machine she found there – a treadle Singer a couple of decades older than her mother's own. There were a few rust spots on its black body, and its chrome was blistered, but the leather cord that drove its wheels was still whole and supple. Jo would say Lex liked to play at sewing, but Lex gave no thought to an imaginary garment, followed no phantasmal cloth through with her fingers. When she sat on her vine-upholstered branch to sew she wasn't being mother, she simply enjoyed the momentous resistance of the treadle against her foot, and the grotto's green, mitigated brightness, its tattered shadows.

Eventually hunger drove her home for lunch. Her father was humouring Jo, who hadn't had to shift her book from the kitchen table, but ate with it open at her elbow, the more recent sentences of her composition hidden by her packet of Lakeland Coloured Pencils. Lex could see that Jo had been forced to make more 'monsters' from their father's scrawls. The book had been his, part of some indexing task. Most of its pages were blank, but on some were scattered stanzas of names and addresses – these Jo outlined, coloured in and gave eyes, ears, mouths and reasons for being: 'Honey and John met a monster. It looked like this.'

After lunch Hester put on lipstick, and her coat with three-quarter sleeves and daisy buttons. She said, 'Be good girls. I'll give Thomas your love.'

On her way back to the grotto Lex found Hayley. Hayley and two other girls were picking gorse flowers to scatter over a bride's head. They had a bowl full of the stuff, some petals crushed to transparency. It wasn't settled who was to be the bride. 'It was *my* idea,' said Hayley.

'But I'm the prettiest,' another girl said – and even

Hayley was astonished by her confidence. Lex saw that Hayley was too surprised to lose her temper. The girl was persuasively dressed in a blue frock with a sateen cummerbund, and white shoes buckled across the instep – these gave off the fruity odour of fresh white liquid polish.

Lex thought it might be more fun to toss petals than be pelted by them. 'I'll do a ceremony. You two be bridesmaids.'

They sorted themselves into a small procession. Lex walked backwards before them. The petals streamed and the air smelled of buttered corn.

'What are you doing?' Three boys had appeared on the stopbank above them. One was around their age, two perhaps ten, like Jo.

'We're having a coronation,' Lex said, already changing the terms of the game.

'King Lippy the Lion,' Hayley added. Weddings were sissy and would shame them.

The two groups regarded each other. If the boys hadn't had some business in mind they would not have noticed the girls at all. Apparently, having made contact, they were at a loss how to proceed. One wiped his nose on his forearm. 'It's your brothers built that fort, eh?'

Hayley nodded.

'They've gone off and left it uncovered. Want to go take a look?'

'I'm not allowed,' Hayley said.

'They're not there.'

'I'll go,' Lex volunteered.

The boys exchanged looks. Lex was a reinforcement, but Hayley was insurance.

'Come on,' Lex said to Hayley.

73

'Me too,' the bride said. 'Shake a leg.' She skipped off ahead of them all.

'She lives in Woburn,' Hayley told the boys – to explain the bride's peculiarities, and her disregard for the neighbourhood's delicately negotiated boundaries.

They all followed the bride, away from the open ground by the stopbank, the field of grass, dock, thistle and low gorse. They came on to a track through the broom. The sun cleared the high cloud and the heat doubled. The whole territory stirred; its tendons popped, then – adjustment made – it lay still again. The children walked single file through mounds of gravel left over from the Council's unfinished earthworks. Lex's father called it 'fill', and it did – stockpiled silence and did away with the usual horizons.

Before the willows and river was another strip of clear ground. And the fort. The children breathed freely again and looked about them. The stopbank had reappeared, a low green wall, nothing visible beyond till the Eastern Hutt hills.

Sheets of roofing iron had been propped up near the pit to make a kind of metal tent, the inside of which was blackened by smoke.

'They've been lighting fires,' the bride said. She stood a good few feet off but still twitched her skirt away from the sooty iron. Lex clutched at the hem of her own pinafore and tried to copy this fascinating feminine gesture.

Hayley and the boys went to the edge of the pit. 'Tunnels,' Hayley said. 'Tunnels, Lex.'

The reports were true. The children climbed down a knotted rope tied to a stake hammered into the ground.

The pit was deep, and five tunnels branched off level with its floor. The sides of the pit were straight, and showed their makers' spadework, neat chiselled cuts. The only untidiness was an occasional grubby, limp lace of fine tree roots hanging out of the soil. To Lex, looking up, the rectangle of sky was an old mirror, silver going a little at the edges – but less superficial than a mirror, a volume of vacancy. And blue; her blue.

David Hough appeared at the edge of the pit. He had either followed them, or had seized the opportunity to make his own investigations. Although he was a trespasser like them, the children snubbed David. He couldn't climb down into the pit, but limped around its edges talking to himself – or perhaps to them, without expecting an answer. Of the tunnels he wondered how far they went, straight or curved. He supposed one or more were emergency exits, or even the exits, concealed. Perhaps he expected the children to collect some of the information he wanted.

The boys had engaged in a debate – whether to explore the tunnels and, if so, who would go first – when something thudded into the bottom of the pit. David put his arms above his head and ran, doubled over. Lex looked up and saw a stone poised against the blue, compact and discrete, like a bird in the shut-winged, falling stage of flight. Something hit her on the side of the head and she fell forward, stunned. She closed her eyes and scuttled into the mouth of one of the tunnels.

The soil was cool and fragrant. Lex looked back from this throat of earth to see one boy follow her. He pushed her forward into the dark and dropping temperature. 'They're coming,' he urged. She crawled on.

Then the tunnel collapsed. Suddenly Lex was caught in smothering covers, stiff rough blankets. A warm ring – the boy's hand – encircled her ankle for a moment, then withdrew. The cold covered her. Soft, friable, airless, overwhelming soil fell between her face and the arms with which she had tried to screen her face – pushed against her eyelids, mouth and nose. A conquering weight pressed down on her body. She thrashed, immersed, blind, suffocated.

And thrashing – automatic now, with no apprehension, no thoughts, only reflex mobility, her last breath gone – her hand caught at something. Something sinewy and firm. A tree root. Lex held hard to this solidity, she pulled herself forward then up.

It was as though light, not earth, sifted down. Grey mealy light. The hole was everything. And pewter-coloured, increasingly coarse grains of crumbled light.

Lex pulled herself out of the earth, hand over hand, and the dirt around her, still tending down, dragged at her body, like peristalsis, tried to swallow her again.

Lex unearthed herself.

Lex lay on the far side of the willow and listened to the sound of a rout. When the big boys finished throwing rocks, the smaller children swarmed out of the pit and scattered. Hayley's brothers singled Hayley out. Lex heard one shout, 'Scrag her!' then scuffles, a shriek. David Hough called out, 'Wait!' then went under – Lex heard body-blows, the grunts of attacker and victim.

Lex lay still. Her eyes and nose streamed. Each breath stank of earth, or of nothing, the air that had no savour, until, as her sinuses filled, she came to smell only the soapflake stink of snot. Lex lay where she was till the big boys saw the children off their property and didn't come back. Then she began to wipe at her face, where there was nothing now, no mask over her eyes or nose or mouth but air. She scoured with her palms, as if clearing clotted web, a memory of obstruction.

At the river Lex cleaned up; took off her sandals and squatted in the shallows to wash her legs, arms and face.

The sun had gone behind the Western Hutt hills. On the far bank the scar of quarry drained of colour then put itself forward, like something nasty in a ghost story staring at a small girl, the hem of whose dress dipped into the water, then dripped. The river moved but made no sound. Lex looked up at the bared rock, and if she had been a rabbit she would have stopped chewing. She stilled; then realised it wasn't the rock that watched her.

David Hough stood on the river bank twenty feet behind her. He didn't say anything, but seemed relieved when she turned to face him. Relieved to recognise her, as if, till then, his inventory wasn't complete. He raised a hand to hail her, an unimposing wave that didn't climb higher than his breastbone, then he turned and bobbed off through the willows.

Lex went home. It was dusk, and though the lounge was alight with pale aquatic television radiance, there was no light in the Keenes' kitchen.

Lex paused in the kitchen doorway. Her mother was there, standing at the sink, in the half-dark, peeling potatoes. The cold tap ran and Hester's hands were red to the wrist. Her eyes were red too.

Lex took a step into the room, but her mother failed to notice her. Lex went forward another step to identify the jumble of whiteness on the kitchen table. Jo's bird bones, she thought. Then she saw it was the collection of rocket parts, capsules and stages. The objects gathered what light remained and glowed like – perhaps – the sky coming apart in mealy pieces.

Lex went to the bedroom and shut herself in, left it dim. She fetched her hairbrush and sat, feet tucked under her, on the end of her bed. She began to brush the earth out of her hair.

PAREMATA

1

We find our subjects by subtraction, no matter how grand those subjects might be. Lex Keene, lying on her back on the lawn on a summer's night, would choose, from among the many, one star from which her saviours could come. That one, blushing above the pines on Big Hill, a place for her faith, the centre around which she could build her story.

On the last day of 1969, Jo Keene and Cathy Brent arranged to meet for a swim. They were good friends but, at thirteen, had an intimation that the conditions of their friendship would become difficult at the start of the new school year. For it was then that all Paremata School's class of Form Twos would have their carefully negotiated codes of kinship diluted by the huge populations of a variety of urban and suburban colleges. Jo and Cathy *had* meant to make the most of the time they had left. But it was several days since they'd seen each other.

'Dad says Christmas is a time for families,' said Jo. 'He gets ideas and sort of *experiments* with us. This is the first time he's been stuffy about Christmas – I wasn't even allowed to ring you before now.'

'I'll have to bring the little girls, I'm looking after them,' said Cathy. 'So you might as well bring Steph.'

'And Lex?'

'I meant you and Lex – if she wants.'

'OK. We'll meet at our end of Brown's Bay. We can go diving off the *Champion*.'

In the late afternoon, Cathy and the 'little girls' walked around the Bay then sat down on the concrete cylinder which covered a drain near the high tide mark.

Cathy's seven-year-old sister Felice chattered, as Cathy tended to Rachel's cap. Felice cocked her head, flicking the matted waves of her hair from side to side and kicking her calloused heels against the drain. She was beautiful, and completely conscious of her own charms, her husky voice, creamy skin and triangular face. Because of this self-consciousness her charm had an edge, her smile was always sly, like that of a child in a fashionably sinister *fin de siècle* portrait.

Cathy helped Rachel stuff her fine, fair hair under a bathing cap. Rachel too was seven – fastidious and timid, she was not at all like the Brent children. She had been an adoptee of Joy Brent for the past half-year. Her father was sorting out his life, job, some woman, and had left Rachel in Joy's care – Rachel and his collection of Samurai swords. These were tucked away under Joy's couch and out of bounds – though the kids would dabble their hands in the dust to touch, and recoil from, the plaited leather and layered steel.

The Keenes arrived, Jo and Lex, Steph trailing them like the tail of a sad dog. Felice rushed up to the plump, whingeing Steph and took her hand. 'Let's go now, so they won't overtake us so fast.' Rachel joined them and the three hurried down to the water.

Lex didn't know whether to follow the younger girls or to wait for Cathy and Jo. At ten, she wasn't necessary to either group but was included in the games of both, proficient in the different dialects of childhood and early adulthood. She waited while Cathy rearranged the discarded clothes and towels, putting shoes on top of shirts in case a wind came up.

Jo stood with her shoulders hunched and arms crossed, hiding her immature breasts. In the months following her thirteenth birthday, her tidy child's body with its low centre of gravity had elongated like a field flower making its bid for the sun. On land she was unco-ordinated, her tendons a size smaller than her bones, all operations at the mercy of the dishevelled control-tower in her skull. And so she liked to swim.

The younger girls were already thigh deep, wading out to the wave-chewed post that marked the place where the seabed shelved into deeper water. Felice and Steph made sounds of disgust as, at each step, the muddy sand, gelid and living, ran up between their toes. The mud was from a new development, Whitby: several fresh empty roads, fully equipped with streetlamp-lined footpaths, that fingered their way into the yellow-grassed groin of a valley above Brown's Bay. The roads cut up into clay cliff faces that had bled into the inlet all winter till cauterised with spray-on lawn: grass seed in a weak mixture of sand-leavened cement.

The older girls caught up at the marker and Cathy, with years of practice, threw herself forward from the last place her feet could touch, and swam.

The water in the channel at Brown's Bay was opaque, green, flat calm and tepid after a month of sun. The flotilla of girls set out into this deep water. Cathy, fat and buoyant, sang as she swam, a song from the Brent kids' new record: 'I close my eyes, pull back the curtain, to see for certain, what I thought I knew . . .' Jo was swimming underwater, going down for half a minute at a time and coming up somewhere unexpected, like the conning-tower of a diving shag. The little girls kept close together, dog-paddling furiously behind Lex, who swam on her back, feet kicking and hands rocking at her sides. All headed for the *Champion* which lay at anchor, turned into the sluggish current, afloat on its own reflection.

Jo surfaced, her hair in her eyes, and said, 'I saw something down there!'

'Probably a conger.' Cathy was cheerful, knowing whoever said would be less afraid than those who heard her say it.

Lex imagined the eels' thick grey bodies and milky marble eyes. She drew her knees up to her chest and, being short of body fat, sank. When she resurfaced, spluttering, she started to swim more briskly towards the *Champion*.

Rachel burst into tears. 'I want to go home!' she cried, as she always did when surprised into distress.

Usually no-nonsense with bawling little kids, Cathy made exceptions for Rachel. This hadn't escaped the notice of her sister, and as soon as Cathy and Rachel turned back, Felice began to scold, 'What a baby you are!'

Steph, swift off the mark since she hadn't wanted to go swimming, was already wading out on the shore-side of the post. She stopped and asked, 'What's a conger?' – cautious, but not alarmed.

Cathy escorted the other two children back to the shallows, where Jo joined them. Lex reached the *Champion* and hauled herself out of the water on one of the flanges jutting from its stern, where a dinghy would be suspended when the launch was at sea. She knelt up on the abrasive non-slip paint and looked at the others. Rachel was clinging to Cathy, arms around her neck and legs around her waist. Cathy called out, 'Come on!'

Lex looked down into the water; warm to a depth of ten inches, then cooler, denser, the deep water that pinched her feet. Somewhere below was mud or sandgrass, and sunken drums of wrecked home-made mooring buoys, shanties for eels. She imagined their beaked, panting heads and tiny teeth.

Squinting at her sister's huddled figure, Jo shouted, 'Don't be a sook!'

Lex heard, across the distance, Jo explaining to Cathy how she, Lex, had always been a crybaby; how she remembered that when Lex was four and they were blackberrying in the Hutt, Lex would shriek if they put her down among the bushes. Daddy would have to carry Lex piggy-back. Or

85

how, only last winter when they climbed up into the forest on Big Hill, if Jo left her Lex would panic and run calling 'Jo!' as though the pines were dangerous.

(The blackberry bushes had been high and thorny; they hid her from her family, swallowed their bodies. The bushes had secreted night within their snarled vines, and the same gobs of colour in darkness that cruised out of her wardrobe when the light was switched off – a door to the deep ocean's glowing, drifting monsters. The pine trees were a deserted cathedral, deconsecrated, astonishingly silent – the silence active, an infestation, a wasp that laid its eggs in the live body of her mind.)

Lex could hear Jo trying to strike the right tone, amused indulgence, but her voice sounded gleeful and smug. Then she heard Cathy calling out to her that *they*, the Brents, would have to go home soon. Joy was going out; Cathy had to make dinner.

Joy was divorced. Cathy cooked for the Brent family – her mother, brothers, sister, and Rachel – three nights a week. She propped up a recipe book to remind her, then never looked at it. She talked to her friends if they were there and plunged out of the kitchen every so often to settle disputes, shouting like a television mother: 'I want you to have your baths now!' Or: 'You'll eat what I cook!'

'Hurry up, we're going!' Cathy yelled at Lex. To Jo she said, 'You can come to dinner.' Then she assured them, 'If we leave, Lex will follow us.'

They began wading to shore, stepping delicately because of the jagged shells in the silt-saturated sand.

'Mum's going to a party. She's wearing her mantilla – it's a black lace veil with a crown,' Felice told Jo. 'She's going to give it to me when I grow up.'

'Why should you get it?' Cathy was indignant.

'*You* wouldn't look any good in it, Cathy. *You* don't have olive skin.' Felice caressed her own cheek – coloured, smoothed, illuminated by her own legends, like vitamins – the youngest and most beautiful princess, the exotic, the love-child. Felice's father was a foreigner and a partial cause of her mother's divorce.

'Jo, if you come to dinner you can meet Pavel,' said Cathy.

'Who's Pavel?'

'He's staying with us. He's a count, and he's staying with *us*,' Felice said. 'We think he's a White Russian.'

Even Steph looked interested. She stopped whining about getting home in time to see *Lancer*, that this week there were Indians, and asked, 'A real Russian, like spies and cosmonauts?'

Jo was scornful. 'White Russians are Czarists – they left after the revolution, before it become communist.'

'When did it become cosmonauts?' Steph asked.

'*Communist*. A long time ago. Is Pavel old?' Jo asked Cathy.

'No, he's Mum's age,' Cathy said, then added uncertainly, 'I don't think he was born in Russia, but he does have an accent.'

'He's lovely.' Felice clasped her hands and lifted her eyes, a little Madonna.

'Is he going out too?'

'To the party? Yes, they all are.'

The group were now in ankle-deep water, close together, setting the stage for the fun they would have. To them,

Pavel was storybook, an exiled prince, a mysterious stranger. Jo thought she would be afraid of him.

They walked out onto exposed sand stippled with crab holes. Steph stopped and looked back across the water at Lex standing brown against the white slatted windows of the launch. She waved. Lex didn't wave back. Her hands were in front of her and her head was bowed. She looked like the African chief from *Best Loved Verse of the American People*, chained in the marketplace.

The others had left the beach. They were walking up the footpath of new white cement, under the sparkling taupatas. The sun had gone behind the point. Its shadow was a stain which spread on the water, feathery edged, about to touch Steph's feet. Steph looked back at the *Champion*. Lex had disappeared. For a moment, in her fear, the bay seemed to tilt, and Steph's vision contracted to the size of a sliding bubble in a spirit-level. Then she saw the bobbing dark head in the water between the launch and the marker.

It wouldn't happen, Lex told herself. Surely she would have heard of it happening if it was at all possible. The bay quaked with her heartbeat. She could conjure up the conger's touch – its thick, multi-joined body, stuffed with muscle, a variable curve; cold; a clinging brush across her shin; its bite, two V-shaped serrated blades sawing her skin; its weight; its thrashing . . .

Then she forgot the eel, the water. She rose from the sea like steam. The bay was a flipped hourglass.

A balloon had appeared above the trees on the point, sailing slowly as though following a line in the air. It was yellow and red in broad vertical stripes, tapering top and bottom. With the sun shining through it, the balloon was a Chinese lantern. Lex saw, briefly, a plume of pale flame, the heat against the sky rippling crumpled cellophane, and heard its full-throated, blow-torch roar. The balloon hitched higher and crossed the bay above her. She heard its basket creaking, heard voices (the host of the air), saw a distilled shadow, darker than a cloud's – like nothing but the shadow of a balloon.

Steph waded out to meet her. They dawdled back up the beach together, watching the balloon till it was the size of a fingernail. Then, shawled in their towels, jandals wet and squeaking at every step, they hurried back up Paremata Road, towards home.

2

The Keenes' house stood next to the Brown homestead, at the intersection of Paremata Road and Oak Avenue above Brown's Bay. The Browns were still in residence; Mrs Brown, a deaf octogenarian, and her remaining (or, as Frank Keene once quipped, *remaindered*) daughter Miss Brown, with her finger-waved hair and floral bib apron. The Keenes' house was built with timber from a demolished wartime barracks at Pauatahanui. Frank's only improvement so far was to replace a porch, held together more by bougainvillea than by nails. Frank was proud of his new deck, but did miss drinking his morning coffee in the purple gloom of the old porch while watching rats run up the thick vines to the gap where the bougainvillea had prised the iron up from the eaves.

Cathy, Felice and Rachel waited, dripping, on the new deck while Jo dressed. Jo soon reappeared, pulling on a cardigan, her hair towelled dry but unbrushed. As she bolted for the door her mother chased her with a comb. 'Come here, your hair's a bird's nest.' Hester Keene patted her daughter's sleeve, testing for a handkerchief, then passed Jo her own. 'Do you want to take a key? Do remember to leave as soon as Joy gets home.'

Jo's father lay on the couch listening to Beethoven. Frank Keene looked detached, reflective, a little ill. That afternoon, down in his workshop at the back of the garage, he had been trying to unblock the vacuum cleaner. The blockage was in the only sealed join in the hose. He tried fishing down the tube with wire, and bashing it against the ground. He tried reversing the flow of air, swapping the hose between the two outlets. Placing his lips over the end of the hose he tried blowing. His cheeks stretched and air was forced, stinging, into his sinuses. He felt something give a little and switched on the vacuum's motor to suck the blockage back into the machine; but the flow was reversed and instead a big clot of dust shot into his throat. He gasped with surprise and it lodged; thick and prickly –

– he was alive alive a river turned aside in its course backed up in ripples as big as mountain ranges. His heart had the unbrooked vitality it had had at sixteen, his sweat popped free of his flesh as it did when he was newly ripe, having his top teeth torn out, without anaesthetic, by a doctor in the tropics. His sweat flowed as freely as it had when he was grubbing gorse on the section in Wadestown where they built their first house –

– tools, tins of paint gaping, the garden craning in at

91

the window. Then he coughed up the clot – coughed, retched, spat grit. A tap dripped. Beyond the glass a fantail flirted in the lower limbs of the fig tree, flipping its tail like a kid giving the fingers. The clot was partly grey carpet fluff, but was mostly made of ravelled strands of his daughter Lex's long hair.

Jo joined the Brent girls and Rachel on the deck. Cathy said, with mock generosity, 'Just as well we're a bit late really. They'll be ready to leave, so we won't have to watch while Gillian farts around.'

Jo asked who Gillian was.

'Pavel's wife,' said Cathy dismissively.

As the Brents and Jo departed Lex and Steph arrived, Steph broadcasting: 'They left us.' Then to her mother, 'When's dinner?' and, worried about the duration of the symphony, 'Daddy, *Lancer* is on soon.'

'We saw a hot air balloon,' Lex told her parents. Once said, the words inscribed themselves in her faultless internal calendar: 'New Year's Eve 1969, a hot air balloon, red and yellow, I was in the water.' She went off to change, in her listening cast that others thought was dreaminess. Really, she was counting revs, the exhilarating engine of her intellect.

Hester Keene set the table. She watched her husband. When he'd told her what had happened to him she'd said, 'If you were really in trouble I would have heard you.' To her it seemed her husband and children were constantly present, like phantom limbs, or pins marking troop movements on the map of her body.

*

Steph wholeheartedly enjoyed *Lancer*. She was right about the Indians.

Johnny Lancer, the fiery son with the thick black bangs and silver bosses on his hip-hugging belt, was shot at by rustlers while out riding range. One bullet creased him and when he came to he couldn't see. He was blind. Indians found him. There was a young woman who cared for him. He touched her face and said she was beautiful. She was mute, not whole, so didn't have a husband. She fell in love with Johnny Lancer and had her brother and some other braves help take him home. She stayed to nurse him. The doctor, who had a Scots accent, string tie and fob, suggested an operation, a new procedure. It was performed and Johnny's eyes were bandaged. Hannibal Lancer sat downstairs with his older son – the fair steady one. The mute Indian girl came down from Johnny's room and put her hand on his shoulder. Her brother and the braves arrived to take her home the day the bandages were to be removed. The sun shone on Johnny Lancer's lips as he told her he couldn't wait to see her face, he loved her, knew she was beautiful. You could see that she was frightened that when he saw her he wouldn't think she was beautiful at all. She went out of the room as the doctor and Hannibal Lancer and the other steady son came in. She got on the horse her brother held. The bandages were unwound, Johnny Lancer blinked at the white counterpane, the filmy curtains, the frosted flowers on the shade of the table lamp. She rode away between the braves. Johnny Lancer happily called out her name and, 'I can see.' 'She's gone, son,' Hannibal said. She rode straight in the saddle as though she knew everyone was watching her think her own thoughts. Johnny

Lancer ran out of the house calling her name. She pretended not to hear him, biting her lip like a woman who could speak and wouldn't. Johnny Lancer christened his new eyes by crying on his father's shoulder.

Frank switched off the television. 'Oh for the days of *The Westerner*. Right, Boss?'

'Yes,' Hester agreed. 'That was pretty poor.'

Seeing her father about to put on another record Steph suggested, '*Carmina Burana*, Daddy.'

This was vetoed by Lex. 'Put on *The Planets*, Dad.'

Halfway through the 'Mars' suite Steph jumped up to conduct. Lex joined her, shoving her sleeves up past her elbows. They conducted each other's conducting like cartoon sorcerers slinging spells.

'You should stay still to listen to music.'

'But this is fun.' Lex was getting better at returning his serves – her father's 'should's were no longer as impelling as physical laws.

'All this throwing your body around – this *expressive appreciation* nonsense. That's the way Joy Brent would listen to music.' He got up and demonstrated, stretching and twisting, covering his head with his arms, pretending to cower from terrors or yearn for light on the horizon. He was dancing. It was clever and funny, also full of malice. Lex considered: malice as mixer, with a dash of pique – how had Joy Brent offended him?

He stopped dancing and sat down. 'But, of course, Joy's a hippy.'

Hester was sitting in the dining room, under *Hunters in the Snow*. In the painting peasants, hunched under game-bags or bundles of sticks, walked down a snowy slope among their thin hounds; below, children skated on an iced-over pond; beyond them a series of snowbound villages receded to the horizon, church towers pricking the blue smoky sky against which three rooks hung frozen like flung stones. Hester was sewing a hem, brows lifted and top lip caught under bottom teeth, indifferent to her husband's lesson.

'This is how a man like me listens to music.' His hands folded on his chest and face composed in angelic profundity. The martial music parted around his expression like steam around a spoon; it divided, both girls heard it become two musics – Holst's 'Mars' suite and a signature tune to their father's homily. Their mother completed the picture, lids lowered, brows raised, something happening behind her expression – the back of the mirror.

3

Sunday. Lex woke to the noise of the three heretical lawnmowers – one her father's. The curtains were open, Steph gone. Lex lay in a tank of light, under a ceiling daubed with ripples. Everyone was outside, virtuous in the virtue of morning sun while she lay in her wrinkled bed, arms thrown above her on the pillow. With no one to attend to, and no daily agenda, she lay still and enjoyed her own emptiness, feeling unfinished and full of potential, like a new subdivision: quiet streets, buried power and phone cables, pricy parcels of land destined for development and occupation – a waiting, habitable space.

Her mother came in, followed by a cat, back arched, up *en point* as it smooched the edge of the door.

'Come on, pet, get up, I'll want those sheets soon. You're

wasting a lovely day. Your sisters have gone out already. There are sausages in the oven.'

Lex got up and dressed. In the kitchen she switched on the grill over the sausages. She could hear her father at the corner of the house, rinsing out the grass catcher. She heated her sausages quickly, so that their skins were black and flaking while the meat was still cold and congealed on the inside. She took them onto the lawn to eat. Her father was lying in the shade on his banana-lounger, a metal tulip thrust into the lawn beside him, its red enamelled petals cupping his beer glass. His eyes were closed. He heard her sit down beside him and became aware of the smell of scorched sausages.

'It's nearly lunchtime, Lex.'

'This is my lunch.' (This is my breakfast, my lunch, this is this out of the way.) Above them branches bobbed, thick with green walnuts.

Lex asked, 'Have Steph and Jo gone to Brents'?'

'I suppose so.'

'Where's Mum now?'

'Around the side of the house cutting wandering willie back from the drains.'

'Do I have to do the dishes?'

'Your mother did them.' Drops of sweat zigzagged their way down through the forest of hair on his chest. His whiskers were sand imbedded in his skin.

'I didn't use a plate.' Lex rubbed the remaining pork grease into her forearms; the dry decayed blisters of her sunburn disappeared.

'Your father –' he began, and that far into the sentence she could tell he'd say something serious, not by his grave

97

tone, but because he always opened any subject of which he was uncertain not by saying 'I' or 'me', but by waving some title like a red cape and standing sideways behind it. 'Your father nearly died yesterday.' He turned his head and looked at her – the one he would gradually feed his fears and adult secrets, the one he had loved irrationally since she was a fierce, greedy baby sucking his wife's nipples flat. He told her what had happened, plainly, the opening sentence a hard act to follow.

She watched him. He made her think of a coin dropped in deep, cold water; and of her short reach; and of the cancelled heat of her own hand reaching, out of its range. 'Don't,' she said. 'You should be more careful.' It was almost the same thing Hester had said, containing 'How dare you' and 'I can't always be there'. Then, responsibility dropping from her like an oversized dress, she said, 'Daddy,' and put her hand into his. She wondered how he could occupy his huge body, surely he must spend his time flying and perching from his hands to his face to his feet.

Lex took a bag of apples to Brents', hoping to persuade her sisters that they wouldn't need to go home for lunch. They could spend all day in Brents' bush.

There was an acre of it, accessible by steps carved into the clay bank behind the complex of house, shed and chicken coop, and by a track that entered the manuka at the boundary of the back lawn where there was a small barbecue pit – charred ground and a ring of river stones. The 'bush' was a hill with a grassy ridge, up which a track ran to a fence and stand of pines. The east slope of the hill was covered in pine, the east valley a forest of macrocarpa, shading bare ground gritty with their litter. The west slope was pine till halfway down, then manuka. Manuka, mahoe, kohuhu filled a narrow valley on either side of the fold of a dry stream bed. Further up towards the boundary were hawthorns, a dead plum tree and thicket of gorse.

Halfway up the steep shingled drive Lex met Glen and Andy Brent. They were sitting in the long grass on the narrower verge, across from the tethered ram, which jerked its head up, mouth working on a beard of grass. It stared at her through coin-slot pupils.

As an excuse for giving the ram a wide berth, Lex went across to the boys. She asked, 'Are you waiting for Gary and Peter?'

The elder, Glen, squinted at her. He had blue eyes and fair skin marked with big pale freckles, like water sprinkled on the surface of sifted flour. 'That's right. We'll be up in our fort today.' It was as good as a calling-card: *The Misters Brent will be home today to visitors after eleven.*

'I think we'll be in ours too.'

'You'll never get the *girls* away from Pavel.' Andy seemed to have forgotten Lex was a girl.

Behind her she heard a ripping stitches sound and the chain stirring, as the ram tugged up a mouthful and took another step. Her back arched, but she didn't look around. 'All of them?'

'I think Cathy and Jo are feeding the chooks. But the others are playing with him.' Andy looked sulky and full of contempt.

'What's wrong with that?'

'Well – Pete and Gary are coming. Aren't we going to play wars?'

Glen and Lex exchanged glances, and then they were playing. Lex felt Asa's ponderous caution in her answer: 'We aren't at war with you.' She was an adult.

Andy was still entirely himself: 'But war is what it's *about*, dummy.'

Then Glen – Sib – also careful: 'Perhaps you'd like to call a truce. For peace talks.'

'And the truce can be a trap.' Andy's enthusiasm had him on his feet and swiping at bushes on the roadside. 'We'll take your representatives prisoner!'

'We can't do it now that you've *told* her, you dork!'

'We could still meet – in an open place where we could see you weren't armed and we weren't outnumbered,' Lex suggested.

'Maybe.'

'Are you two playing right now?' Andy had caught on.

'We have to do this again up in the bush. It can't have happened here – this isn't anywhere,' Lex said.

Andy grabbed Lex's arm, then remembered she was a girl and dropped it. 'You have to get those other girls away from Pavel.'

Lex went on up the hill. She didn't anticipate problems. To Felice she would speak about housekeeping the fort, or dress her for one of the Shaman's ceremonies – knot her shirt at the front and thread a flower through the knot. Rachel would want the same, for the sake of camouflage becoming Felice's twin. To Cathy Lex would say, 'Shouldn't we renew our devotions up at the waterfall shrine?' And let her choreograph some new rite . . .

The door was open. She went through the glassed-in patio that connected the new lounge to the older cottage.

Opposite her, out the door that led to the back lawn, she saw a girl she didn't recognise, a big blonde girl, full breasts and hips stuffed into a floral print mini. The girl was sitting on the lawn beside Joy's deckchair. She had her legs tucked under her and was gnawing on a lock of her long hair while chatting to Joy. Joy wore cut-offs, sunglasses, and a tight smile of manifest patience.

Then Lex heard, from the split-level lounge, her younger sister's voice reading, thrilling and ludicrous: 'A sailor's wife had chestnuts in her lap, and munched and munched; "Give me" Quoth I – '

Another voice, a man's, breaking in: 'No, darling, the O is the same as it is in *broth. Q* as in *quick*. Do it again.'

Lex climbed the stairs.

The little girls were kneeling in a semicircle about a dark-haired man. They were all reading from the book he held. Entranced.

Pavel, the first to feel watched, looked up, brows lifting, ready to repel with friendliness anyone out to poach his fun. He saw a child, a girl; surmised, the third sister – Lex – not the moony, gangling one with breasts growing. She stood, one heel still overhanging the top step, watching him with an alertness that made nothing of their inequalities. For a moment he was sure they wouldn't be friends and he wondered how she knew not to be charmed.

He lifted a hand and beckoned. *From a marble balustrade; a gilded sleigh; the rail of a white boat gliding into a crowded river landing; from the back of a horse blowing steam* – in a land starved of such gestures except as delicacies in its cinemas the Count hailed her, 'Come and join us,' his voice so welcoming that she could see herself there already, kneeling, closing the circle.

'We need a man of action. You look like a man of action. You can read Macbeth.'

Lex stayed where she was.

'These three are being witches for me.' He said their names, like sweets he rolled with his tongue against his palate. Rachel, Stephanie, Felice.

His hair was dark brown, swept back, his eyes tilted, oiled stones. To include him, the room became a collage. It was Joy's room, with her batik cushions, deerskin hearth rug, carved glorybox, her print of *Starry Night*, and here were Lex's friends and sister, cut from last night and pasted on this morning, but Pavel seemed to come from the pages of the *Listener* – a guest star on *Mission Impossible*.

Lex stared at him much longer than was polite, then looked around the room as though she'd never seen it before. 'I was looking for Cathy,' she said; then, to exclude him, 'We're going to play in the forts today.'

Felice said, 'This is more fun.' Yes, he heard that right, she said it as though snubbing a suitor. Lex seemed incensed. Pavel was enlightened – here was someone used to setting the order of business.

Lex heard Cathy in the kitchen, whistling and washing her hands. She went back downstairs, passing Jo. Jo was on her way up, her eye furtive and bright.

Cathy was rattling the soap in its cage under hot running water. She shoved all the dishes onto one side of the sink. 'Help me dry these.'

Lex got a teatowel and stationed herself at Cathy's elbow. She said, 'I have a good idea for our tribe. I'll tell you about it in the fort – once we're all there.' Cathy merely nodded. Lex elaborated on her appeal: 'I think we should spend some of today decorating the shrine. It can be the New Year.'

'They'd have a seasonal calendar.' This was the sort of observation that had earned Cathy the part of Shaman. 'It would have to be a midsummer celebration.'

'Say it's midsummer then.'

'It *was*, about ten days ago.' Cathy fished the last of the cutlery out of the water and went to the pantry to collect materials for the ceremony. Some flour, sugar, paprika and turmeric. As she shook portions of each into plastic bags she kept watch over her shoulder.

'It's OK. Your mum's still on the back lawn with that girl.'

'That's Gillian.'

'She's *married*? Is she old enough?'

'Eighteen is old enough. Not that she's particularly grown up. She's so gushy. Even Rachel gets sick of her. Gillian is always trying to dress her up and do her hair.'

Lex found it hard to imagine Rachel disliking anyone who fussed over her. Rachel craved the attention of older females. She liked to nestle against Jo or Cathy, she'd even feign tiredness or fear just to get their arms around her.

(There had been tears, jolting shouts, but no one heard her calling. No one came. She fell asleep and woke in the early hours of the morning – went out to find her mother on the floor in the kitchen. She lay down too with her chewing nappy pressed to her cheek. *Mummy, Mummy*. But her mother was cold as the lino, cold as the kitchen whiteware. Rachel had mimed herself at three years old, shaking a heavy, unresponsive body. Lex had listened, watched, her brain a black aperture eating shaped light. She recorded Rachel as Rachel told her story and, telling, asked the world to be tender to her.)

'Cathy,' said Lex, 'we have to get the little kids away from Pavel.'

'They shouldn't be bothering him anyway.'

Lex was about to point out that Pavel was the instigator of the game they were playing, but stopped when she realised Cathy was about to barge upstairs and tell the children off. She followed Cathy, who stopped at the top of the stairs with her fists on her hips. 'You kids, Pavel probably has better things to do than entertain you.'

Jo, sitting on the couch and pointing at the group with almost every end or angle of her body – nose, chin, hands, knees, feet – said, 'Cathy, I don't think they're . . .'

'Look, we're all going outside to play, OK?'

'Katerina, love – ' Pavel said, amused and chiding, 'we are having a wonderful time together. You and your friend should join in.'

'*I'd* like to,' Jo said. 'I've read *Macbeth*. I'll do anyone, I don't mind who.'

'On a day like this we should all be outside,' said Cathy.

Beyond the two women on the lawn Lex saw the boys, with a machete and new bamboo spears, walking into the bush along the bottom track. *Their* territory. She spoke through Cathy's crooked arm. 'We need someone to follow the boys – there they go – and spy out a place for a parley. Those spears aren't part of their arsenal. They're going to hide them somewhere, I bet. I want to know where.'

Enthralled by her sister's voice – Asa's tone of command – Steph got up, volunteering.

'Good. Stay with them, leave signs, don't get caught.'

Pavel sighed and pinched a page corner between his fingers, rubbing the paper till it creaked. Then he closed the book and got up off the floor simply by unfolding. He rose with the burdened grace of a camel coming up off its knees.

Cathy, apologetic now, repeated, 'We should be out in the good weather while it lasts.'

'It seems set to last forever, sweeting. This interminable hard heat.'

Lex, liking its sound, mouthed – palmed – Pavel's last phrase. *Interminable hard heat.* Jo stared at him, jaw loose, imagining him dressed in white furs and striding towards her over sugar-icing snow.

Steph jogged onto the track among the manuka. The sun needled through the foliage, piercing her eyes in periodic flashes. The boys weren't far ahead; they talked in volleys, panting. They were jogging too; Steph could hear the metronomic slap of their jandals. She rehearsed the signs she could remember: a split stick showing that a party had divided; an arrow of stones pointing not to the path anyone had taken, but always forty-five degrees to the left; a circle scratched in the dirt to show if they were lying in wait somewhere up ahead, dots in the circle to show how many . . .

The boys were keeping to the left of the stream bed, even where they had to wade through a deadfall. Steph was puzzled. They were respecting the Shaman's curse and so must be playing, but she could hear them still using one another's names: 'Pete,' 'Glen,' 'Jeez, Gary – '

She waited till they passed the lodge and began climbing the hill. Then she crossed to the easy side of the stream and lay down near the lodge to watch them scramble up between the pines.

4

A month earlier, on the last day of rain, when the lodge was half built, Cathy had laid her curse on the stream's crease and dared the boys to cross.

The girls went out when the trees were still shedding water. They lit a fire in the barbecue pit at the head of the bottom track and cooked up manuka tea. They carried the billy to their lodge. Felice unravelled the Shaman's robe from around the ceremonial bowl. A Chinese bowl with an orange and gilt glaze, it had once stood on the dresser in the girls' room, filled with hairclips and hat elastic. Cathy strained the tea into the bowl and they passed it around, sipping, and sniffing its resinous steam.

They sat, religiously silent. Rachel remembered lying

peacefully across her father's lap with her face turned in against his shirt, chewing on one of his buttons as though it were a nipple. Cathy fought through ranks of pictures that wouldn't be still but billowed in her face as if she walked through rows of clothesline strung with coloured clothes and white sheets – set nets catching schools of light. She was six. She was sitting in a church in a foreign country, looking at candles as pretty as lacquered nails and painted statues miles more real than department-store dummies; a man at the front was saying a long poem that settled over all the things she wanted to touch and taste, like her Nana laying white gauze over the lunch so that flies (and children) couldn't get at it. Felice thought about the ballet lessons she would take next year and the pink leotard she'd been promised. Jo worried about walking up the drive to Tawa College for the first time, with all the other turds – without even an older sister or brother as an aloof spectator on the bank or ranged in D Block's top windows. Steph, infected by the others' reflectiveness, relived the wonderful shivers she'd had watching an episode of *Voyage to the Bottom of the Sea* – one about the ghost of an evil U-boat captain and his haunted submarine – hearing the deep sonar echo that had the Admiral turning to Lee and saying, 'Empty vessels make the most sound.' Lex thought what she always did: *What can happen?*

The boys came down the hill. They had mud on their arms and legs, and red headbands high on their brows pushing their hair up into crests. They carried bamboo spears with sharpened, fire-hardened ends, and didn't approach stealthily, but appeared bold, painted, and in full view. They meant to invade the girls' lodge.

Rachel saw them first: four painted figures, skin dark and ulcerated, eyes shining and crystalline in their scaly, mud-daubed faces. Rachel was frightened; Glen had fixed her ponytail that morning, but now he looked not at all like a brother. She said, 'Savages!'

Then Jo: 'Invaders.'

'It's only the boys,' said Felice, not stubborn, just slow. But she too was caught in the traces as the team moved forward. Cathy rose to the occasion and jumped across the stream, her teal robes swirling about her ankles as she landed flat-footed and emphatic, facing the invaders. Behind her Lex got to her feet and called out a challenge that pulled all of them through into another world where these people were their deadly enemies: 'You were not given permission to approach our village!'

'This is sacred Agawa land,' Cathy croaked. 'Our ancestral homeland.' She threw back her shoulders and raised her arms. 'Trespass only at your peril!'

Pop-eyed Gary, a mild bully at school, sneered at Cathy and tried to share his sneer with the other boys. Pete and Andy looked to Glen for a cue. Glen went pale; his freckles stood out, mottling the unpainted patches on his face. '*Cathy?*'

She struck herself on the breastbone. 'I am Osto Drin, Shaman of the Agawa!'

'Lay a curse on the stream, tell them they'll die if they cross it,' Lex whispered.

Cathy turned away from the intruders and passed her hands back and forth over the stream bed, gestures she had learned watching *The Magic Hands*, then she spun to face the boys. 'There! Only the Agawa can walk on the ground on our side of the stream. If you Others walk on it you'll die, your bellies will fill with fire, your faces will go black and smoke will pour from your eye sockets.'

Jo, eyeing the spears, told the little kids to get behind her. Although she was enjoying the confrontation she was, as ever, in two minds. They glared at her, conscious of the fact they were now Agawa warriors (Steph), nobility (Felice), or at least general members of a populace who expected both to be protected *and* to have to make a loyal stand.

Steph saw that Lex had one hand behind her back, fingers wiggling. She picked up a small cone and pushed it into Lex's palm. The hand closed.

Glen was saying to Cathy, 'It won't happen if we don't believe it.'

'Don't be spoilsports. You have to pretend to be another tribe, don't you see?'

'That's not what I mean, ah, Osto, what I, Sib – ' he blushed, ' – chief of the Others, am saying is that, since we believe something different it won't happen to us. Your curse doesn't have any power over us.'

'You have no respect,' Cathy puffed up.

'Yeah? So we'll smash your statues!' Gary yelled.

The shrine was a game. In a cave of soft rock cut by a small stream and floored with scalloped silt deposits the girls had made four flour-plastered blue-clay statues. A clay woman reclined on a branch of the hawthorn that grew jutting out above the floor of the cavern; there was a cat, and a bird, and a clay snake wrapped like rata around the limb of another tree. The cave struck home every pitch of Lex's voice. It was a *game*, their deities, their made-up mysteries.

But.

But Lex suspected she was cheating. Everything was in one piece, her family together again after five months uncoupled and, it seemed, lying in sidings – last year, when Dad was selling the house in Wadestown and Mum and the rest of them were living in their uncle's bach at Waikanae. Now Dad had a new job; to celebrate the girls were each allowed half a glass of red wine. Toasting him, Mum had seemed so happy. She was filling out again, showing off the tops of her freckled breasts in a new, splashy, patio-print sundress. Next year's promises: a company car, and Grandma's own-your-own up the Gold Coast. Lex's world was in one piece, in good order, not just working order. Then there was her father's creed to consider – that atheists were valiant, gallant, sitting down with their deaths at breakfast lunch and tea – a faith to which she was a postulant. She had walked out on an argument with a friend's Christian cousins saying, heroically, 'God is just a crutch, and an insult to a big, complicated universe.' Yet she felt that perhaps she was cheating, running a race with a head start, and soon disaster might begin gaining on her, or might simply smash the shell of the sky. And so she soothed herself by making clay idols and settling them in tree branches.

Lex ran past Cathy crying, 'You infidels!' She threw the cone and charged up the slope. The cone sailed across Gary's head. Gary drew back his spear arm – Glen, several feet away, lifted his hands as if to catch hold of it – and threw the spear, which flew, wobbling, and struck Lex on the shoulder. She fell backwards, her feet off the ground, out of her jandals. They could see how small she was, all the personality and determination of her climbing body reversed. She landed on her back, flipped over, slid and fetched up against the trunk of a pine tree. Jo, Cathy, Steph and Glen all converged on her. As the girls picked her up she used them to frame her as she faced Glen. 'The shrine is the source of the stream, the stream is the border of a tapu place . . .' Her voice was groggy. A thread of blood outlined her ear and began to trace the course of a vein in her neck.

'You're bleeding!' Steph said, more impressed than worried. Lex felt for the blood. She touched her scalp at the back under her hair, then she stretched out her arm and printed three bloody finger marks on Glen's forehead. 'That seals the curse!'

He was astonished. The blood was warm for a moment after her fingers withdrew, then the wind touched it and turned it cold.

Sib decided his tribe should retreat, respecting the Shaman's curse. But Gary disagreed and crossed the stream, where he stood for a minute with his arms folded, facing Cathy. Lex sat outside the lodge smearing the cut on her scalp with spit from her fingertips.

Several days later, Felice confided to Steph what had happened when Pete and Gary stayed over for dinner. Cathy was cooking, and while Felice was in the kitchen helping her serve she saw Cathy pour a cap full of pink Swirl into the sauce on Gary's spaghetti and meatballs. Gary was a guest; he struggled to eat at least half the strangely soapy food – and spent the evening queasy, then downright ill, his belly full of fire.

5

The Keenes' move from Pomare to Wadestown in 1967 hadn't worked out. There had been a year's anticipation, rides by train and bus out to the Mairangi Road section, where the girls watched their parents grub gorse and helped carry bunches of it to the fire with hands gloved against prickles, fat spiders and centipedes. When the foundations were laid, the frame raised and clothed, the girls were sent off to play, out of the workers' way, but they were allowed to carry home, as a memoir or appetiser, a lump each of window putty sweet with linseed. Then came the shift. They were bundled off to relatives while their home was dismantled and reassembled in the new house. The girls arrived in Wadestown to find their beds made and rugs spread the same as ever, clothes, shoes and toys arranged in cupboards – everything familiar, but drenched with the unhomely smell of new timber and fresh paint.

Adjusting to Wadestown was difficult. Jo disliked their new school. The primers and standards were segregated not by a field or fence, but by streets. The morning assembly ended in a regulated march to classrooms to band music piped, tinnily, through speakers suspended above the top playground. The girls had to learn not just to drop in on schoolfriends, but to telephone first. At Pomare they simply used to walk around the back door (front doors were never opened), knock, and ask if Sandy, or Naomi, or Charlene and Kerryn could come out to play. Once Jo overheard her new friend Rosalyn's mother saying to Rosalyn, 'I don't like that girl. She's vulgar. She has a horrible journalist's accent.' It would have been hurtful if Rosalyn's mother could be taken seriously, but as often as not when Jo saw her she was propped upside down against a wall, legs folded and forehead sunk into a cushion – or was on the phone telling some friend that to eat the meat of butchered animals was to consume flesh filled with the fear of death.

In Wadestown Hester discovered she was afraid of the wind. The way it would come charging up the valley to assault the hillside on which their house was built. One day shortly after the move, when she was stooped over the greasy clay of her protean rockery – a garden in which her choice of plants was confined to tough natives, succulents and daisies – she looked up through the hair lashing her face and saw the roof where it had been only loosely bolted to the eaves lifting and dropping some two inches. Each night she would lie awake for hours listening to the wind

114

fingering every seam and join, as patient and compulsive as a child turning a puzzle. Many nights, so as not to disturb Frank, she would sleep in the kitchen, the most firmly anchored part of the house, on a foam rubber mattress laid on the floor. Days when the children were at school and a strong wind was blowing, Hester would roam around the house, unable to sit down or concentrate on any of her tasks. This wandering was so shamefully unproductive that she took to knitting on her feet, the skein tucked under one arm.

The night the storm came she lay on her mattress in the kitchen feeling the whole house straining upwards into the gulf of sky, its nails vibrating a little looser every minute. Then there was a crash and the house shuddered. Hester called out and Frank appeared. He looked into the lounge and saw the house was holed; the wind was inside, reading every magazine in the room.

As they hurried to dress, the second crash sent them running to the other end of the house. Hester roused Jo. At the door of Lex and Steph's room Frank stopped to collect himself, then went in to find them standing at their window peering out at the silver dragon that had alighted on the garden. He took them by their arms and drew them away from the window and the flying iron.

While the girls breakfasted Hester kept watch at the window. The roofing iron rolled like a length of cloth off the property and over the road where it wrapped itself around the thick leg of the corner mailbox. She saw iron like thrown drapery sail past from the house above them. Ceiling tiles fluttered down the valley, white, like pages torn from a book.

Two days later Hester saw that the road below her house was littered with winnowed treasures the wind had taken for chaff. There were playing cards and snapshots and crumpled bits of dried toetoe, there were fragments of a jigsaw map of the world: the Arctic islands of Svalbard set in pack ice coloured yellow on the map; a piece of the Pacific at latitude 40° south; and a blue thread of river that changed its name at each border.

After the storm Hester took her daughters to live with her in Waikanae while Frank put their house on the market. For the girls Waikanae was a fairly easy adjustment. The school was small and dominated by two huge families, each with eight members dispersed between Primer One and Form Two. The playgrounds were taken up by lunchtime rugby practices – so the girls clotted together in a small space between the climbing frame and a patch of concrete painted with hopscotch, four-square, and games with bubbles and ladders that no one cared to play. After school the motelier's daughter would stand at the gate and solicit: 'Come over to our place. It's five cents for half an hour in the pool or twenty minutes on the trampoline . . .' And on pet day the children would produce not just budgies, dogs, cats, mice and the occasional tame opossum, but lambs, calves, ponies and piglets that squealed like whistling kettles.

On Saturday mornings the girls would walk the mile to the Newman's Bus stop to meet their father. He would buy them each an ice-cream with half a Flake thrust in the top of the cone and a gumball bleeding blue or green into the ice-cream at the bottom. They would try to fill him in on all the week's events. How Lex had a teacher who said he had a Roman nose, 'Roamin' all over my face.' How Jo had invented a game called 'Battling Bull' which Mummy hated them playing indoors. How Steph had a pet slater called Dubcek, after that man they were always talking about on the radio.

Hester, Jo, and Steph were happier when Frank was there, but for Lex his arrival was always haunted by his departure. Weekend nights she would wake up from tangled dreams waking couldn't quite comb out and sit up into the patches of light, hot and yellow, shining through the hedge from the incubators of the next-door poultry farm. She would hug herself and rehearse her memories of all the things she believed she would never know again: that walk along the elevated, green road on top of the Hutt stopbank; playing on Taita Drive in pyjamas on a summer evening; frost sticky on the bars at the head of the right-of-way; builders' tape tangled in the powerlines of Mairangi Road, snoring in the wind; afternoon light through her bedroom's blue-and-white gingham curtains. Sometimes, remembering these things, she could find her lost world simply by shifting her gaze from the memory to its environs – although really here she was in *this* bedroom, with other bedrooms one or two clicks back on the Viewmaster. Sometimes she found her memories of the lost world had been snatched away: a piece of furniture, an hour of the day and angle of the sun, a tree, the height and shape of a doorhandle. Then the lost world was a loosening mesh in which she was still safely caught, beyond which was everything else and what would happen, everybody else and what they had to say.

Early in the new year the Keenes moved to Paremata. There they found, once again, a whole new set of customs and rules to contend with. On their first day at school, Lex said to her teacher, 'I'm on spelling level eight.' She was on level three. And, 'With all these shifts my swimming certificate hasn't caught up with me – but I'd just won the last sticker.' If riches couldn't be transported, then disadvantages could stay put also.

6

Once everyone began to co-operate it turned into a good day, full of spying and the interpretation of signs and secret messages. At midday the tribes agreed to parley. On information gleaned from Steph's spying the girls discovered a cache of spears fastened with a slip-knotted rope to the branches of a tree. They retied the bundle, made a granny knot. In late afternoon the parley took place, then dissolved into a quarrel as the Others had intended – but when the Others reached for their hidden spears they had to fumble to free them, giving the Agawa delegates and their body-guards plenty of time to escape down the hill and across the stream.

Shortly after six Jo made damper and, to amuse the little kids, dyed it with red and yellow food colouring. They cooked it on the barbecue coals while Cathy and Lex refreshed the shrine's statues and symbols – fingerprinted three-petalled flowers made of flour paste dusted with paprika.

Before eight, the Keene dinner time, the girls hurried home around the Bay. Jo dawdled, head down, having let go the trapeze of sociability and dropped into sullenness. Steph and Lex walked on the shore, over rocks with a papier-mâché finish of dried sea-cabbage, rousing the herons who balanced in the shallows, beaks in the water, playing pick-up sticks with their own reflections.

Dinner was lettuce parcels. Lex watched Steph consuming greater quantities of fresh vegetables than she could normally be persuaded to eat. She saw that their mother had devised the dish for this purpose, and realised that for years she'd been tricked into eating as a treat things she professed not to enjoy. Steph hadn't caught on yet and it was fun to watch her tuck into *yuk* raw spinach, *yuk* radishes, *yuk* spring onion – all things she would normally sift out of a salad of sliced tomato, shredded lettuce and grated cheese.

As they ate Jo talked between and around mouthfuls about Pavel. She continued to do so when she and Lex were washing the dishes: how wonderful he was with 'the children', his deep voice, his huge hands; how she bet he had a hairy chest.

Lex spent the evening reading in her room. When she'd finished her Andre Norton novel she closed it and lay back on her bed. As she thought about the story all of its ultimately resolved possibilities came back to her as they had first appeared – the only unroped-off passages in a mansion holding an open house, a guided tour for the imagination.

A silver rocket set among the turrets of a palace; caverns hiding hundreds of maimed renegades; a jewel that picked out its wearer as special. A fine thing that. If only someone would give her a pendant that glowed whenever she alone wore it. It almost seemed possible. The book's images spilled out between its closed covers – an over-filled sandwich. Tomorrow, she imagined, she would be approached by a stranger, a man with wonderful eyes and no sign of hair on his face. He would hand her a jewel, a stone as warm and living as a mouse. He'd say, *This, by rights, is yours. Others will try to take it from you at their peril. It will uncover hidden roads and lead you alone on marvellous journeys . . .*

Lex wasn't finished with the world of *Stargate*. She wanted to read another story about the same people, or the same story in which different things happened. She decided to write it herself.

It seemed to her that the first thing about writing a book was the book itself – twenty sheets torn from a jumbo pad and creased in the middle, a cover of Christmas wrap, cut to size. She went out to the lounge to ask her mother if she could use the sewing machine to bind her book.

'The bobbin isn't threaded, and I'm not getting up to do it now. You'll have to wait till tomorrow.'

'I want to start it tonight.'

'Why don't you write on scrap paper?' her father asked.

'Because it wouldn't be a book then.'

'Tomorrow,' her mother repeated. 'Don't you want to watch *Randall and Hopkirk?*'

'No,' she said, but she did.

Her father said, 'A book is what you write, not what you write it in.'

'It has to look right.'

'And this is the girl whose teachers complain about her handwriting. Who is going to be able to *read* this book?'

'Pipe down, Boss,' Hester told her husband. Lex's face had gone white. Wasn't that child ever going to learn how not to be drawn? Jo at thirteen could be expected to be weepy and bad-tempered, but Lex had always been thin-skinned. If, an hour later, she was asked what she supposed her father had been doing she'd say, cool-headedly, 'Just teasing me.' It was as if she wouldn't, rather than couldn't, see she was being baited while any argument was actually in progress.

'Go and tell Jo *Randall and Hopkirk* will be starting soon,' Hester said, and Lex went off obediently, letting the argument end there. She was, fortunately, very suggestible. For instance, all that Hester ever had to do, in cleaning even a nasty cut, was to say, hiding her own desire to flinch – 'It really doesn't hurt that much, does it?' and Lex would agree, 'No, not much.' Her mother's words were more persuasive than the signals of nerves in her injured flesh.

Jo had hung her coats on the outside doorhandle to stop the door slapping against its frame. Lex pushed the door open. The light was off and the darkness full of the concentrated silence of stilled breathing. Lex sniffed the air and let the door fall shut.

In a city of felled willows roofed with ivy, across the Hutt's stopbank – the result of the County Council's long delay in converting the river flat from groves of willow and blackberry to a field of grass – Jo had learned a trick from an older boy. One day when they were together in the bath in the grey-and-white bathroom in the new house in Wadestown, she taught the trick to Lex. She persuaded her sister to sit facing away from her and lean back against her tubby, tubular torso and open her legs. Jo wondered whether this joy was standard – would it work for Lex too?

For a while they did it to each other, Jo in particular relaying instructions: 'Harder, faster . . .' They called the result being 'frantic'. Lex would ask a gasping and quivering Jo, 'Are you nearly frantic?'

After a while Lex stopped letting Jo touch her but might do it herself after doing it to Jo. Later she stopped altogether and when pressed she told her sister that she only did it to *herself* when by *herself*. After that Jo had to work her pleasure into their games, perhaps proposing, 'Hermes has been sent by Zeus to torture Hera.'

When they were living in their uncle's bach at Waikanae they would go down to the bottom of the long, grassy section, past the lemon tree with its lumpy-skinned lemons, their dry inside rinds as thick as flutter-board. They would crawl through the fence and into the tunnels that honeycombed the base of the cutty-grass hedge. Jo would set the scene in the game, then pull off her trousers and lie on her back concentrating on the always too fastidiously light and slow touch of her sister's fingers. She was twelve, Lex nine. It was beginning to feel different. Lex would get exasperated with her because she couldn't stay still and would bully with urgent instructions.

Lex understood that Jo was different from her, but not

that *this* was becoming different too. Then one day, as she watched her hand moving above the flushed folds, the clenched inverted heart of buttocks and flexed legs pushing up from the floor carpeted with dun dust and flakes of dead cutty-grass, she saw a drop of clear fluid squeezed from the slit below her hand – not pee, clear and more oily than pee – slowly dribbling down into the crack in Jo's bum as she became frantic.

This game continued for a short time after they shifted to Paremata. Lex wanted to end the game, but she could offer no good reason to give up and she thought Jo would treat her reluctance as a lack of generosity. But it had begun to colour things: that ripe smell between her sister's legs, the down lengthening and darkening there; Jo's disappearance, *her* disappearance for Jo, in the moment before Jo became frantic; the doughy flesh pressed greedily up against her hand; the ribbon of fluid ever more pearly and viscous, scented, savoury and acid like some tropical fruit.

One evening she spent working at Jo's pleasure, while hidden high in the branches of the macrocarpa hedge at twilight, when radiance and darkness were separating like an egg yolk and white. Below, the lawn was a basin into which shadow-stained air slowly drained. The windows on the near side of the house had their curtains drawn, white lining like a sudden growth of pallid fungus filling the rooms, stuffed up against the glass. All these things, the twilight, the twining smells, because of what she was doing seemed changed in a miserable, threatening way.

At the next invitation Lex said, mildly, 'No, I don't want to.' And Jo never asked again.

7

Three days after New Year's Eve matters had altered between the Brent children and their mother's guests. Gillian and Felice had become the best of friends. The seven-year-old and the eighteen-year-old would sit in giggling conference in the corner of the living room, absorbed in a code of catch phrases and simpers filtered through their fingers. Gillian had begun to encourage Felice's sisterly conspiracies against Andy.

Felice Brent sometimes felt that she was not just different from her brothers and sister, but excluded by that difference. There was very little she could do to assert herself. Teasing or telling tales were the usual weapons of the youngest child, but were no use against Cathy and Glen.

Cathy was too much in favour to be told on, Glen generally too well behaved. Teasing left Glen unruffled and Cathy amused. Andy, on the other hand – bumbling, perpetually hungry – was a good target.

Jo Keene observed Gillian counselling Felice on strategies for goading her brother. This behaviour was fuel for her fantasies: *He sees how immature and unworthy she is. He notices me. That I* – and here the wishes would sprint away into dream situations: Pavel a moral man tormented by guilt at his liaison with an underage girl (statutory rape – the odd, evocative name conferred by television programmes). Still, she and Pavel would have several wonderful weeks hiding out from the police in some backblocks bach, and she'd make an impassioned speech at his trial. When she came home her parents would be gentle and deferential, and would never treat her like a child again . . .

Though Gillian's conspiracies with Felice were a cue for her daydreams, Jo also found them disturbing. How could an adult behave like that? Setting one child against another? They weren't her children; it wasn't the same as when their father cranked up the debate between his daughters – then, when they became upset, began to play the impartial judge, chanting his usual litany: *logic; objectivity; there is no black and white only many shades of grey.*

Joy Brent was unaware of any escalation in the usual squabbles between Andy and Felice. There were so many demands on her attention. It was the holiday season and she had her hands full of her charity cases, various unattached male acquaintances, men Joy was convinced couldn't survive without her mothering. Rachel's father came and camped one night on the living-room floor, on the far side of the room from Gillian and Pavel's makeshift bed. He sat outside all the next day in a pair of denim hipster shorts, reddening his tan and reading books on educational theory, while Rachel lay nearby making daisy chains to decorate and transform him.

Jerome Bradley, Joy's boyfriend, the last scion of a local landed family (after whom a bay and long flat-bottomed valley had been named), lounged around sipping gin from under a lid of lemon and checking his watch. Joy prepared lunch for their drive and, on the side, made a pot of soup for Cathy and Jo to take over to Sam.

When Joy had departed and the tide was right out, Cathy and Jo carried the pot wrapped in a tablecloth around the Point to Ivey's Bay and Sam's bach. He put the soup on his stove to heat and took them to see his hidden still – the clear liquor draining into one of those big antique bottles other people filled with arrangements of dried flowers.

On their way back Cathy told Jo she thought her mother was wrong to think Sam needed looking after. 'Being drunk is part of being a poet. It isn't as if he does it by accident. That still must have been hard to build.'

'You know what people say? They say that Jerome and Bruce and Sam are *all* your mother's boyfriends.'

'Which people?'

Jo made a short list, omitting her father, who had said it more often and with more spite than anyone else she'd heard or overheard. Cathy's mouth had gone as broad and lipless as a frog's. Jo said, hastily, 'It wouldn't matter even if it was true. I think people say that because she's more lively than they think she should be.'

'That's right. Because Mum's divorced they think she should be unhappy. Sometimes I think people believe being unhappy and being respectable are the same thing.'

Jo considered this, wondering whether she was wrong in thinking that being unhappy made you *important*. In stories special people were always specially unhappy, stuffed with alluring and momentous sadness.

It was hot. The air between the hills and the harbour was agitated with heat; beneath their feet the muddy sand felt sticky like the pastry on the inside of a pie. By the time they reached the top of the drive their throats were well powdered down.

Cathy made them a milkshake. While she stood at the bench adding ingredients with exaggerated sprinkling and pouring gestures – the Shaman's theatricality overflowing into the everyday – Andy came in to sneak biscuits. Without turning from the bench Cathy kicked the pantry door shut and held it closed with her foot, saying, 'No, Andy, lunch is in an hour.' He continued to complain and struggle with the door, so she began to chant a limerick she sometimes used to embarrass him into submission:

> There once was an Indian called Andy
> Who went in the pub for a shandy
> He wiped off the froth
> With his old loincloth
> 'Blimey!' said the barman, 'that's 'andy!'

Andy burst into tears and ran out of the room. Cathy, stricken, chased after him. She shouted, 'What's wrong? I *always* say that.'

Andy fled along the bottom track into the bush. Cathy came back and began to apologise: 'That boy's losing his marbles.'

'Felice has been teasing him all day,' said Jo.

'But they're always on at each other.' Cathy switched on the blender, her face webbed red.

Frank watched his neighbour George Just bouncing between the barbecue and the bar, slick, dressed down, professionally jovial. With George everything was salesmanship; there he went, putting across the family man. Hester, her head tilted to listen through the shrieks, gabbling and music (*Yummy, Yummy, Yummy*) was talking to a woman in a dress chequered like a finish-line flag. Frank sipped his whisky and water and looked with habitual lazy curiosity into the hollow shadow up under the woman's dress, between her fleshy thighs. He was a spectre at the feast, the neighbourhood barbecue, in its sunshine; its smell of chlorine billowing up off the pool; its sounds of sizzling fat, and spirited conversations about gardening, rates, television programmes, kids, and its careful conversations about politics or work, all decencies observed. Hester seemed happy, he thought, as though she'd lived thirty-nine years to mix with people like these. He had put in his time making conversation, being pleased about his new job, his career advancement. He was now ready to leave. He turned away an offer of cheesecake (soft sweet and sour grease on gingernuts crushed and dampened with sherry), saying, 'I'm not really a man for desserts.'

Hester called out, 'Frank! You must take your just desserts.'

George laughed loudest of all. Frank smiled to show that he at least knew what they thought was funny, and went to the edge of the patio to stare out over the harbour, the high-finance Seaview Road prospect. Flourishing his difference like an opera cape, concealing himself from all of them.

George was being the teasing Kiwi salesman, not a flatterer, but a joker. Laying on little outrages to put his guests at ease, George served his feast of beef and ribbing – laying in goodwill.

A group of children rushed past Frank and jumped into the pool, and George came up beside him. 'You should have brought the kids over for a dip.'

'They're all off somewhere. Probably playing war games up behind Joy Brent's.'

The children climbed out and jumped in again, eyes squeezed shut and kicking the air in luxurious recklessness.

'Your oldest girl must be going to college next year.'

'We got her into Tawa, despite the zoning – she has cousins there. It has a better academic record than Mana or Porirua.'

George nodded. 'Very important.'

'Jo will do all right as long as they manage to interest her. All my children are very intelligent, but Jo's attention tends to wander.'

'It'll be two more years till I have to make a decision about Neville.'

Despite the reverberating din from the pool, Frank could still hear those highly specific civilised sounds: ice cubes rattling in glasses, a battery of steaks sizzling on the grill, the jangling guitars and wire brush drums of a Top Twenty song. Here he was, discussing his children's education with a stationery salesman who had just mentioned Rathkeale.

George added, 'Of course I left college after School Certificate, what about you?'

'I was at St Pat's. Expelled in the fourth form.' Frank wore his past rakishly.

George guffawed and clapped him on the shoulder before going back to the barbecue. Such familiarity. George was fortunate that he, Frank, had come so far from the days when he would not have permitted any of the casual touches and hearty slaps with which he believed men tested each other by trespass. He had been such a mean bastard, the man no other man could touch. The miseries of his childhood had left a residual charge. Even now Frank thought of his anger as the genie in *The Thief of Baghdad*, huge and unmanageable if it were ever to escape, if the stopper were unwittingly pulled from the bottle. He doubted whether his anger, like the genie, could be duped into shrinking and re-entering the bottle, to be shut away, to beg and promise its obedience and service.

When Andy had finished he immediately felt hunted; his breathing was the pack rushing up around him, echoing back off the walls of the cave like a held breath blown out of a scuba diver's snorkel. The pick had left claw marks in the moss-covered mudstone. The water wouldn't run clear. Small branches were broken off the hawthorn leaving feathered stumps. The statues were lumps of clay dissolving in shallow water among scattered red berries. With a last look at the ruined shrine he scrambled out of the stream bed and ran to find somewhere to hide.

Cathy and Jo, drawn outside to investigate the shrieking on the front lawn, found Pavel playing chasing with Felice, Steph and Glen. Rachel watched them while still leaning against her father. After briefly considering how full of milk their stomachs were, Cathy and Jo joined in. Rachel abandoned her father.

Jo felt sufficiently camouflaged by the children to offer herself as prey for the stalking Pavel. He treated her exactly the same as the others, was just as inclined to pretend to hunt her and swing on someone else, or ignore her and wait for her unwariness. Twice he caught and tickled her with the same innocent glee he would show on catching Glen or Rachel. And, because she was ticklish, Jo would laugh and hunch over struggling just like the others. She couldn't muster seductive calm; but she *did* feel different when he was touching her, as if she had stepped out of a fast elevator. She couldn't resent him for thinking she was a child; she wanted him to be loving, upright and pure.

The game was interrupted by the sound of a powerful engine muted by an equally effective muffler and the thousand striking matches noise of gravel gouged backwards behind tyres.

'It's Dad! He's got the Porsche!' All the Brents ran to the edge of the lawn. Red, low-slung, streamlined, dimmed by dust – it was Bill Brent's new millionaire brother-in-law's Porsche. Bill opened the driver's door and leaned across the car's roof, one foot on the ground and the other planted on the plush carpet under the dash. 'Who's for a drive?'

Pavel straightened smiling and Steph, his latest catch,

pulled away from him grinning happily. Her soft arm, terminating in a pudgy damp hand, slithered through his fingers like a dropped necklace. 'Goody!' she said, hurtling away towards the next diversion. Bill waved to Pavel then was busy with the logistics of fitting himself and six children into a sports car. 'Cathy in the front passenger seat – you're broadest across the beam, love. Felice can sit on Jo, Rachel on Glen. Where's Andy?' Bill got all the way out of the car and strode towards the house calling his younger son.

Andy had climbed to the top of one of the pines along the boundary fence, holding the tapering trunk between his hands and knees. Now he hung, legs wedged between some of the flexible top branches, plastered in patches of black resin, swaying in the breeze and looking out over the harbour. Paremata – a curling line of P-class yachts rounded the Point, following the path of the channel, tacking or canning, a flourish under its signature. Within Andy's sight there was no bare or sparsely covered earth, from this angle no lawns or shore, just tree and roof tops, the harbour and – directly below him – dark flounces of pine boughs.

He heard his father calling his name, a rare voice, a promise of treats or praise. Andy forgot his fear of punishment, and his plan to punish the others by staying lost till everyone came looking for him. He began to descend gingerly, bellowing, 'I'm coming, Dad!'

While Hester put her cuttings in water, Frank fossicked in the litter of booklets, paper and pencils Lex had left at the end of the dining table. She had still been working when they had gone out to the barbecue.

'Do you think she remembered to have lunch before she went?'

'No, not a proper lunch, but you'll find another row of the caramel square missing,' Frank guessed. He opened the book covered in Christmas wrap. Lex had filled twenty pages with printing, her light pencil pressing hard. There were about ten words to a line and fifteen lines to a page; each page was copiously illustrated. The story so far: detailed descriptions of the physical appearances of human and animal characters, and a narrative full of sudden theatrical disclosures.

There were several other booklets among the litter of coloured pencils and cut-up magazines. Each one said 'Passport' at the top and had a variant of the NAC logo at the bottom. Frank called out to Hester, 'Is this passport game new?'

'I don't know.'

He opened a book and read aloud: '"*Name:* Aron Chatharat. *Address:* No fixed abode. *Occupation:* Jewel Thief. *Description: Hair:* Copper. *Eyes:* Violet – " Violet! Why not mauve, cerise or indigo while you're about it?'

'Pardon?' Hester reappeared.

Frank continued turning the pages, then, evidently delighted, said, 'This passport has a "Life Story".'

'She probably thinks passports do.'

'Listen to this. "Aron Chatharat was an illegitimate child. He was brought up in a monastery. He was to take all the vows to be a monk but the day he was to have had his head shaved he ran away. He was sixteen by now and old enough to work. He was a thief and an arsonist and got jailed for fourteen years but escaped after two days. He joined a gang of Mexican counterfeiters and got caught but escaped to Cuba. There he did something, we don't know what . . ." I guess that bit constitutes his mysterious past, ". . . that got him a death sentence by firing squad. But he convinced the firing squad that if they killed him he'd haunt them for life. He escaped from Cuba with the help of Russian agents. BEWARE, he may be charming but is really a dangerous man. He is very sneaky and I *advice* you to take care checking him and his belongings." And this person has a passport?'

Hester was pleased Frank's mood had improved. On the walk back down Seaview Road he had seemed determined to have her agree that the Justs weren't really worth their time and effort. He'd even said that he felt politeness to dimwits compromised his standards. She'd laughed at his loftiness. 'But politeness to hosts is essential, surely.'

'Well, I didn't enjoy myself.'

'Enjoyment is a talent of mine,' said Hester.

Frank so begrudged the necessary kindnesses, like courteous attention to the conversation of others. Hester wondered how they would get on if she behaved that way too. It was unthinkable. She didn't have the right to be bored or disaffected. In her it would be considered unattractive, outrageous, some sort of disorder.

She lit a cigarette and said (she couldn't help herself), 'I'm glad your mood has improved.'

Frank waved a hand as if casting something behind him. 'George Just disgusts me, all that hail-fellow-well-met stuff, his La-Z-Boy furniture, and oil paintings of storms at sea.'

Hester found herself turning away from her husband and heading into the kitchen in search of something to do. He embarrassed her. Those harsh judgements were a result of insecurity, she reminded herself.

'Well, Boss, we can't all be abattoirs of good taste,' she said, and he went to correct her before he caught himself. She bit the end of her cigarette so had to stub it out against the damp sink.

She flicked the butt out the window through the withered bells of the abutilon. She wished she didn't have to calm herself by practising 'that bloody pop psychology', as Frank would say. This habit she had of explaining things to herself was a pretty poor refuge against anger. Particularly when her memory of Frank's scorn invoked another memory – of the context of his derisive remark. His version of an old trouble of theirs. She was reminded of the old hurt, of its unearthly vitality.

When I confessed to you about my affair and you made me stop seeing her then used to keep me up all night going through those bloody pop psychology books trying to work out where we'd gone wrong. It was that – all those late nights sitting up drinking black coffee – that gave me my ulcer, you know, and then I was forced to go on that high-fat diet and ended up weighing fifteen stone. Which suited you.

Frank's march of reasons. All the turns he took in the maze of her unforgiving nature, her ambition to understand what had happened – for God's sake – to *another* person after all, between two other people. A sinful ambition, Frank believed, like building a tower to God. Yes, Hester thought, a tower, a place to ignite a high light which would shrivel shadows of excuse and illusion. Or, at least, her urge to understand was an instinct to inspect the injury, to assess the damage and plan the course of treatment. But Frank resented this urge, and of the whole episode what he remembered best was his resentment: *her* voice chasing away sleep, *her* books found on forays into public libraries for contemporary nonsense, *her* coffee, *her* ulcer flowering in his stomach – turns and turns taking him to this terrible place: a house in a Gold Coast suburb, three daughters, so many rights curtailed, even his right to be disagreeable threatened.

8

The Brent house was still, glittering in its baked garden. Pavel lay on his back in the mottled shade under an elderberry. The corners of his mouth were wet, the double row of eyelashes usually seen in male infants made shadows on the soft skin covering fatty bulges beneath his eyes. As Lex stood looking at him he woke and rubbed his face, dragging his mouth down into an exaggerated scowl. He looked at her and said, '*To je to vztekle dite.*'

'What?'

He closed his eyes again. 'My head is full of broken statues.'

She pictured this: the dim green of a vine-hung garden and shattered statuary. She asked, 'Where is everyone?'

'You are so businesslike.' He leaned up on one elbow.

'Joy is on a picnic. Gillian has taken Rachel's father floundering. Everyone else is on a drive with Mr Brent, excepting me, I am here.'

'Is it all right if I wait for them to come back?'

'Certainly, Alexia.'

She frowned at him, fine muscles bunching between her eyebrows, then turned back the way she'd come.

Five minutes later he tracked her out to the front lawn. He had two glasses half full of ice cubes and an opened bottle of Fanta. He scanned the lawn and the flax bushes lining it – perhaps she had gone back to the foot of the drive to wait. Then he felt her stare, a pressure around his neck like a noose, making him raise his head. She was sitting on the house roof, arms clasped around her knees, against the bright slope a stony shadow, like a gargoyle.

'Would you like a cold drink?'

'No thanks.'

He felt foolish, standing with bottle offered and ice melting. 'So, you would rather sit up there and sizzle like a fish on a skillet?'

'It's not so hot.'

He lowered the bottle, its glass slippery, sweating cold. 'What is wrong with you, Alexia? Why are you so unfriendly?'

'I'm not thirsty, that's all.'

He shrugged and went back to the kitchen, stuffed a cork into the Fanta bottle and placed it back in the fridge. Then he returned to his spot under the elderberry.

A minute later he saw Lex cross the angle of the roof and come down to the gutter on the near side of the house. She contemplated the pergola that stretched seven feet between the house and the roof of the woodshed built hard up against the bank. She slipped off her jandals and tucked them into the waistband of her shorts, then stood for a moment balancing, her heels raised off the hot steel, before stepping out onto the upward edge of the one-by-six, her soles curled to grip as she wirewalked to the woodshed roof. She climbed onto the bank and disappeared through the trees' drapery of shade.

He dozed for nearly an hour in the spreading shadow, relaxed, his mind marinating in the chlorophyll scent of the bruised moss in that last damp corner of the lawn, his bones settling snug in his muscles.

Then she was back, announced by the rasp of gritty earth on the sole of a bare foot and a trickle of stones, dry dirt and pine needles. He rolled over. She was on the lip of the bank, above the gouged-out toe and hand holds. He could see that she had just snatched back the foot which had slipped, spilling debris. She was swaying.

He ran to stand beneath her. She was so pale that tiny freckles had put in an appearance, her tan now cross-grained. Her left leg was bent at the knee, all her weight placed on the other foot. She met his eyes, her animosity forgotten, passive with shock. He raised his arms and beckoned.

'Sit on the edge and dangle your legs over.'

She obeyed, trembling as she bent and caught herself on one straight arm. The sole of her left foot was stiff with blood – blood-shod – and still shedding.

'Step down – put your right foot into my palm.'

She extended her leg, her weight still on the bank, arms braced and shaking. His hand closed around her foot.

'Come forward, then let go.'

She shuffled forward, then, feeling herself sliding, stopped her slide by jamming her left foot against the bank. She cried out, lifted the foot out of a dark footprint and fell into his arms.

She was a small, spindly ten-year-old, easy to carry. He took her inside and set her down on the second-bottom step of the staircase. He straightened her leg so the injured foot rested on the back of its heel and, seeing she was worried about making a mess, said, 'Blood will do the tiles no harm.'

'I stepped on a nail.'

There was a puncture in her instep, swollen, the flesh puckering out of the wound where the nail had been drawn forth.

'It was in a piece of wood. It made a *noise* when I pulled it out.'

'Alexia, I will telephone your father to tell him to come and get you. Then I will find a basin and some disinfectant and clean your foot for you.'

The tiredness rings under her eyes were showing dark against her skin. Her expression was wilder than pain would make it, or even the noise of a nail tugging against the suction of parted gristle. Her face was alive with needy confusions – questions, explanations, childish distress seething at him like little flames.

Pavel went to telephone.

'No, Joy is not here. The others are out with Mr Brent. Alexia arrived after they left. No, only me.'

Frank Keene didn't have a car; still, he said he would be right over to fetch his daughter.

Pavel hurried back to Lex with a bottle of Savlon tucked under one arm, a rolled bandage under the other and a plastic baby bath full of warm water. Her teeth were chattering; the skin around her mouth was perceptibly blue. He took a blanket from the rolled wad of his bedding and draped it around her. He knelt on the floor before her and poured a quarter of the bottle of oily, yellow disinfectant into the water. 'Put your foot in that. It will sting.'

Her foot shed grit and plumes of fresh blood.

'Your daddy is on his way.'

She flexed her foot in the water and her breath caught. 'Just let it soak, then I'll look at the damage.'

'Mr – ' she began, then stopped stubbornly. 'Pavel.'

'Yes?'

'If someone wrecked something they thought was yours, because you are supposed to be their enemy, but the thing they wrecked was theirs all along – that's crazy, isn't it?'

'If they ruined it because you were going to take it, that's not so crazy. In times of war a country under invasion will often destroy its own crops, roads and bridges so the enemy can't make use of them. It's called a "scorched-earth policy".'

'No, what *they* did, there's a word for it, like robbing graves.'

'Desecration?'

She nodded. The colour had come back into her mouth. 'Defiling a sacred place,' she said, softly. Words she had heard, but never used.

The red-tinged water grew slowly opaque.

'Things happen like that,' he said, and she looked at him with, he saw, amused contempt – a child wearing the whole world like a garment with an endless resource of pockets, safe places to put sacred things. But *he* knew. The frontiers to his spoiled sacred places were closed. All pockets empty and turned out. From another country he had watched the tanks rattle past the road sign to his last shrine – his home – and had held up his hand as if reaching through the television screen. But he, no child, was unable to imagine the grey metal monsters rearing back from his distant raised hand. Instead the tanks clawed across his hand and rolled up his arm and into his mind – swift fortresses of foreign invasion. It changed him like an illness. The world of his peers was gone for ever. This knowledge imposed on him a kind of second childhood – he was no longer part of his society, he had neither patrimony nor majority.

He lifted her foot from the basin to dab gently at the sole with a wad of cotton wool. She might need stitches and a tetanus booster – he would mention it to her father in case he wasn't a sensible man.

'Tell me where the nail was. I should remove it before anyone else steps on it.'

'Up at the boys' fort,' she said, and blushed.

He stripped the cellophane off the bandage and began fastening a fresh pad of cotton wool in place against her sole.

'Our shrine wasn't really religious,' she said, explaining now.

He nodded.

'It was just a place to put things where I hoped they'd be safe. Not real things, just . . .'

He split the end of the bandage and tied it. He could feel her pulse on either side of the binding in her ankle and toes.

'Next time I'll *invent* a place to put things for safe-keeping,' she said, as though making a memo.

'That's a good idea. Perhaps a cave in a cliff face riddled with caves,' he suggested, and once again he had her complete attention – not the smothering hostility he had felt in her stare when she was on the roof, but a kind of guarded voracity. 'Or perhaps a castle with a thousand rooms and a lock on every door. Rooms you can lock yourself inside, and leave locked behind you when you are away.'

'Somewhere safe, where everything is the way I say it is.'

He smiled sadly. 'Do you believe that's possible? Perhaps you will find signs of others living in rooms you have left locked. Or things won't be exactly the way you say they are because you won't be able to help building your castle out of stones taken from other castles. Perhaps flawed stones. It would be as if you had furnished a house with old, untreated wood, complete with borer beetles.'

'It is possible. I know it is.'

'Are you sure this irreligious shrine of yours is ruined for good?'

She averted her face. 'I'll never go there again.' She had been shaken by whatever she had discovered up in the bush before the nail pierced her. Now she was practising being bereft – getting the feel of grief.

He left her sitting on the stairs and went up into the lounge. She heard the sound of books being shifted, then he came slowly back, riffling pages, finding the right page like a magician shuffling for 'pick a card, any card'. It always intrigued her how adults could do this.

'Here is a poem I think you might appreciate just now.'
He sat beside her. 'It is titled "Inis Fal" – which is ancient
Irish. I don't know what it means.' And he read:

> Now may we turn aside and dry our tears
> And comfort us, and lay aside our fears
> For all is gone – all comely quality,
> All gentleness and hospitality,
> All courtesy and merriment is gone:
> Our virtues are withered every one
> Our music vanished and our skill to sing:
> Now may we quiet us and quit our moan,
> Nothing is whole that could be broke; nothing
> Remains to us of all that was our own.

At the foot of the drive Lex piped up: 'I'm too big to be
piggy-backed,' and Frank had to assure her that since it
was the dinner hour next to no one would be out on the
street to see her. He remembered how, when she was six,
he had decided that she was old enough to go hiking with
him in the hills above the Hutt Valley. Coming home, she
had fallen short while trying to leap over a ditch. She slid
backside first into the cress-topped soup of mud and
emerged with a dark stain on the seat of her shorts that he
knew she was worried might be mistaken for a shit stain.
After all, she was only four years out of nappies and could
vividly remember being 'dirty'. So he let her carry his pack.
It hauled her shoulders back and hung banging on her
calves, but it helped her walk through Pomare with her
dignity intact.

Fortunately, Paremata Road was quiet; only sprinklers

stirred in front gardens, water chop-chopping the evening air. As Frank started up the slope from Brown's Bay, Lex said, her voice muffled against his back, 'Jo says she loves him.'

Pavel, that romantic Czech exile. To Frank's knowledge his eldest's first crush. Frank felt disenchanted, old; it seemed that everything was going to schedule. 'It happens,' he said.

Her voice was sleepy, but not soothed. 'Why do people say that? "It happens", as if they always know what is going to happen.'

'When you get to my age there are a lot of things that just don't hold any surprises.'

'But Jo's never said she's in love before.'

It wasn't general, but particular. Jo had said 'I love' – something Lex had previously heard only from made-up grown-ups on television. Jo said she loved Pavel, and that infuriated Lex, to whom he was an illusion, like God – a mirage, a seductive image of a distant place, a false rumour of water.

'We're nearly home, Curly,' her father said, drawn by her silence. Then, 'You come back to me in twenty years and tell me you haven't said to at least one person, "It happens."'

'Shall I make an appointment?' She laughed, resting her head against his back. 'I'll visit you then, and tell you I *did* stay surprised.'

Through his shirt he felt the shape of her face, warm, a profile painted in temperature – a struck coin, the fortune to which he was held hostage.

9

Vandalism had altered the voice of the stream; it sounded coarsened, ordinary, like a tap running into a cement tub. In her anger Lex had felt her blood carbonated, quickened by an upward, airy torrent. She'd run up the hill and across the ridge to the boys' fort. There she did the most insulting thing she could imagine: climbed up onto the tree-house platform, planted her feet and scooped her shorts and panties aside to urinate on the planks. The urine splashed her ankles and formed a large puddle with fish-scales of oil afloat on its surface. She climbed down and hurried over to a pile of timber to find something heavy – something to smash things with – and trod on the spike of a nail hammered through a board. She tried to jump away from the pain, but the plank moved and knocked her other leg from under her. She sat down. All her vitality burst out of her and drained away into the ground, as though in the moment of injury her body and the soil had formed an electrical connection, a one-way circuit that sucked her hollow.

Lex spent several days confined to the living-room couch, reading and watching afternoon television: the Plasticine men *Filopat and Patofil*, savage moon-eyed Manga on *Kimba, the White Lion*, *Arthur and the Square Knights of the Round Table*, and muttering, fey Harry Worth.

On the second day, Glen visited. He appeared in the doorway, leaned into the room and peered this way and that before coming in.

'Are Jo and Steph out?'

Lex nodded and they blushed at each other. Hester came in to turn up the TV news so she could listen to it over the running water while she peeled potatoes. She greeted Glen, then, Lex noticed, went on to be more hospitable than she would to a *girl* visitor – fetching a plate of hokey-pokey biscuits and two glasses of lemon Quench.

Glen had a plan, one to make things right again so the game could continue. Three days spent making bows and arrows, flicking mudballs, playing scrag and watching TV had made him feel queasy, as though he'd gone too long without eating. He needed to be able to take sides in a story again, to be somebody more important than he was himself.

Glen said, 'Look Lex, Andy didn't mean to upset you or Cathy especially. He was mad because he was being teased.'

148

'I wasn't teasing him.'

'I know. Felice was, and Rachel and me kept laughing. Mum told us off when she found out. And Pavel told me off about the nail.' Glen wanted to show her they were quits.

She looked disdainful. '*He* just turns into a grown-up when it suits him.'

'Fair enough; he is a grown-up. But look – there's no reason why your stuff should be spoiled.'

Lex shrugged. 'It is spoiled.'

On the TV there were pictures of a mass rally in Khartoum. An American reporter was saying: 'President Nasser told the rally that Arabs demanded Jerusalem and the West Bank of the Jordan and the Syrian Golan Heights even before Sinai.'

Lex said, 'The Shaman's magic was part of the rules, Glen. The shrine being smashed up means we were beaten and driven away.'

'But it doesn't have to mean the end of the whole game.' In his eagerness to impart his plan Glen jumped up from his chair and came to sit on the couch, one leg folded under him, facing her. 'Everything would be all right if we could make the Agawa magic come back. I have this idea – we could make it look as though the gods made a judgement in your favour by doing something to our fort.'

'What? Wrecking it?'

'No, look – ' He glanced at her mother and, leaning towards her, dropped his voice. 'You and I could sneak out one night and decorate *our* fort so it looks like *your* shrine.' He straightened up and made a flourish as if expecting applause.

'I suppose we could do that,' she said, without much enthusiasm.

On the TV the fluorescent-bleached, bruised face of Edward Falk, 43, of New Jersey, looked discouraged – as though he could hear the newsreader say that he was listed as serious with breathing complications, two weeks after the Christmas operation in which he'd received the heart and lungs of a woman.

Glen said, 'I didn't mean that we could do it, I meant that Sib and Asa could. They can plan it together, so that my tribe will be frightened into respecting yours.'

'Why would Sib do that?'

'For peace.'

She frowned. 'But if Asa agreed it would mean he was being sacrilegious by faking an act of the gods of his tribe . . .' She broke off.

Glen was staring at her dubiously. 'Is Asa supposed to be a man?'

On the TV a man with a plum in his mouth was saying, 'We are emerging from a decade of dissent and demonstration, a decade of pop, pollution, pot and pills . . .'

'Asa is chief of the tribe. Of course he's a man.'

'What about Osto?'

'He's a man too. Shamans are always men. Aren't they?'

'I don't know.' Glen was baffled.

'They have to be men to do the things they do.' Lex was definite.

'But you make up what Asa does, and you're a girl.'

Lex 'tsked' impatiently. 'Imagining things and doing them aren't the same.' She couldn't imagine a girl doing all those things, making plans, issuing orders, taking things on herself.

Glen shook his head. 'How weird. I'll have to learn to say "he" when I'm talking about you – Asa – to Pete and Gary.'

'I'm *allowed* to be a man!'

'All right, keep your hair on!'

Lex glowered at the television while Glen waited for her to recover her temper. The man with the plum was concluding: 'It is unnecessary to underline the prime importance of being able to see the other fellow's point of view, and even more so of being able to meet him halfway . . .'

'Well, what do you reckon?' Glen prompted.

'I suppose it's worth trying. In a few days, when my foot's better. I'll ring you.'

On the day Cathy told her Pavel and Gillian were leaving early the following morning, Jo came home feeling flat and cheated. At home things were everyday and dreary: the TV talking into an empty lounge; a pair of gardening gloves, kitchen scissors and a bowl full of fresh beans on the bench; an amplified squawk of skin on porcelain as someone moved in the bath; and up on the bank a rustling and thumping as the quinces were shaken down from their unclimbable tree.

Lex limped into the kitchen watching her feet. She appeared to be practising walking on her injured foot. Startled on seeing Jo, she stopped and sat down. 'I'm mainly resting,' she said. 'I wonder what would happen if I walked too far on it before it had healed.'

'It would just take longer to heal. Has Mum started dinner yet?'

'I don't think so.'

Their father came up from the garage carrying the vacuum-cleaner. He said, 'It's fixed,' then went to put it back in the laundry.

Jo said after him, 'Cathy's asked me to dinner at Brents.' Lying timidly.

'He didn't hear you.' Lex was brushing grime from the bottom of her bandage.

'You can tell him for me.'

'Shouldn't you wait for permission?'

'It'll be all right – we were only having cold meat anyway.' Jo headed for the door, looking back warily. Then, because she had always offered her sister confidences which Lex treated largely as entertaining stories, she said, 'Pavel is leaving tomorrow.'

'Good. You can start being normal again.'

Jo said, 'You're horrible.' She hurried out of the house.

Jo avoided the driveway and waded through a gully full of fennel. She waved her way through a pall of midges to creep up behind the house where she knew the little door in the continuous concrete wall of the foundations would be open on its broken latch. She crawled under the house.

Leaving the door open a crack she stayed close to its light, surrounded by a litter of chipped china cups from a child's tea set, and a plastic dumptruck parked among miniature earthworks. As she listened to their voices, for *his* voice, the light faded. Soon she could barely see the boards above her, dry-rot foaming out at their joins. Behind her, through the half-closed door, a strip of deep blue air was all that was visible of the outside.

When the household moved from the dining table up into the lounge, she followed them, into thicker darkness, crawling across the confined space, the hard-packed earth under her hands and knees interrupted occasionally by a block of wood, a swatch of canvas, or a rusty paint tin.

'Cathy, you've got such a big gap between your teeth you could never get food caught there.'

'That's a backhanded compliment. Besides, Felice, you'll probably get a crowded jaw when you grow up.'

'I won't! Mum, I won't, will I?'

'Leave her alone, Cathy. No, Andy love, not *Cluedo*.'

'Aw, Mum!'

'Joy, do you mind if I put on *Ball and Chain*?'

'No! Put on *Joseph*.'

'Surely you kids have thrashed that to death by now. *Ball and Chain* is super, Gillian.'

Music, and their voices coming up out of it every so often like the flippers of seals rolling in a kelp bed at low tide. Jo knew he was there. He laughed once and she knelt up so that her hair brushed and clung to the eczematous underside of a beam. But she never heard him speak.

10

There was a conversation no one overheard.

Gillian wished she could shut up, but the words spooled out of her mouth – love – reversed and dirty, like a typewriter ribbon. She wanted to recall him to her, to have him repeat all his lovely love-sayings: 'Prague is only a small corner of my heart, the rest is yours, a home for you, in which you burn and glow.' The spark in the centre of his gaze.

She said, 'Sometimes I think you married me just to get to stay here. You said you loved me . . .'

'And I do love you.' His words were as by-the-way as tracings left on the sheet beneath a love letter. He lay on his back beside her, eyes glinting, lacquered by moisture as he blinked. She asked, 'Why, when I was singing to you, did you start a discussion about how I loved my love?'

'It wasn't a discussion, Gillian. Since I was the only one speaking it was more of a dissertation.'

They had been drinking coffee, she and Pavel, sitting side by side on the hearth (their empty cups were still there now, just out of reach – she could smell stale milk over the bitter metallic scent of a residue of old ash), Joy and Cathy on the couch. Gillian was admiring her husband: his hands with their tributaries of veins; the symmetry of his soft upholstered collarbones; his hair that without touching she knew was as accommodating as warm water, inviting her to dabble her hand. Enchanted and unguarded she began to sing to him: 'Black, black, black is the colour of my true love's hair.' But, when she reached the line 'I love my love, and well he knows', Pavel interrupted her. 'How delightfully *revealing* that is. "I love my love." That is to love the experience of oneself in love more than the love object. So, when we beg a lover, "Leave room for me to love you," we are really saying, "Don't ruin my love, because I love my love." '

Her hand had dropped from his hair.

Cathy said, 'Piffle. I think you're just saying that because it sounds good. I love my family whether I want to or not. I never think about enjoying it.'

'I think Pavel means romantic love,' Joy explained.

'Well, I wouldn't know about *that*,' said Cathy, sounding like someone declaring that they hadn't read *War and Peace* or *The Lord of the Rings*.

Gillian sat up in the dark and put her face against her knees, heavy-headed with misery, saying over and over the word 'God' – a stone dropped to test a depth. The silence,

Pavel lying still behind her, a house full of six people who must not be disturbed, all abysmal. She asked him, 'You didn't marry me just to stay here, *did you?*'

Pavel's head moved on the pillow. The room was growing lighter though it was two hours from dawn, or so said the clock's glowing pips and strokes. Everything in the room was clearer and Gillian wondered why in her distress these objects were suddenly calling themselves to her attention, lighting up and crowding in.

Her husband wasn't thinking how to answer her, but was remembering her when they first met: the way she listened to him talk; sat on the edge of a big armchair, looking up, angelic, suppliant, serene. He had used all his fine talk and his rich repertoire of gestures, but all his wealth was spent before that first touch past tenderness. Beyond that first touch, all that remained was fumbling impatience, and the heat leaving his hands.

The room was growing brighter. Through a gap in Joy's too small, made-over curtains he could see a low pallid cloud cover drawn up over the sky. The street lights were collecting, reflected beneath.

He sat up, braved Gillian's raised shoulders and the ridged curve of her spine. He put his arms around her and pulled her down, held her antagonistic body. He was angry with her, his lips closed over what wouldn't be soothing noises. Then she turned in his arms to get her elbow under her. She leaned over him, the even ends of her hair swept his neck and all the warmth of her body hurried down its strands towards him. He let out his breath and involuntarily put his hand up to protect his face. He couldn't see her expression; her head was a silver-lined shadow.

'I need to believe I can please you,' she said, with a poetic confidence not to be acquired by reading the right books, a confidence stored with the hoard of summers in her hair and skin and eyes.

'Gillian, I'm afraid you will leave me. Then where would I be?' (Where am I? How do I begin to learn to live here?)

She listened to his tone. It was so strange, not beaten or contrite, his marvellous voice dignified by sadness. Her stranger, her senior . . .

He said, 'Soon we won't have to sleep in our friends' houses. I will be teaching and you . . .'

She put out her hand to stop the mundane assurances that misused his voice – touched his cheek, his palm, his thigh.

Glen got up at midnight to sit at the window of his room. He listened to the neighbourhood doors close and dogs settle, and silence grow in lengthening intervals between each car. The moon came up slowly behind the trees, ushering them forward to stand closer to the house; then it appeared, fat and cold, the shadows of its frowning mountains fully visible.

When Glen heard Lex's stealthy progress along the side of the house he picked up the bag he had hidden in his bedclothes, its paper crumpled many times so it was limp and quiet. He climbed out the window.

Lex had their mission's other ingredient, a plastic bag full of blue clay she had dug at the outlet of a stormwater drain where the pressure of the spout of winter run-off had laid the beach open in a deep gouge.

The two children made their way to the fort, stopping

on the ridge to listen to the distant sound of a train crossing the bridge at the mouth of the inlet.

Lex's foot troubled her on the climb down the far slope. Glen took the bag of clay from her. At the fort he helped her up the ladder onto the platform where they unpacked the flour paste, red paprika, yellow turmeric and bunches of yellow and orange marigolds. They set to work.

As they worked light grew in the forest – moonlight diffused through clouds full of water vapour. Glen became gradually aware of a decay of sound in a night he already thought silent. He couldn't tell what had been subtracted – an intermittent breeze in the foliage, the clank of a hawser on an aluminium mast out in the bay, or the chirruping of katydids. When he looked at Lex, who was absorbed modelling a six-finger hand, Glen saw that her bare arms were covered in goose bumps. And he remembered how, when he was a small child, his mother had carried him to the window of a room that overlooked a park and had stood watching a terrible *something* come and go that made her skin, the skin against which he was held, roughen with gooseflesh.

(Joy went to the window to investigate an odd silence in the street. And, because for several years after the Missile Crisis her dread was habitual, she held her son tightly and shivered as she watched the light grow cooler, pink, and a red-tinged shadow flow across the field. The leaves on the hedge hemming the park, turning colour, seemed to advance from the background, stridently alight, their colour enhanced. Two women, on the street below Joy's window, looked back over their shoulders and pointed at a cloud seeping, a dull red-brown, across the sky.

'It's smoke,' Joy said to her son.

The air cooled. Only thick smoke. Light like a clear rosé charged the glass of air over the city. Only daylight under the shadow of smoke.

But that evening, Joy read in the newspaper how, at eleven forty-five in the morning, the moon's shadow had grazed the sun.)

Frightened by his memory, Glen said, 'Let's finish Lex, it's really late.'

Lex wiped her hands on the empty paper bag. She appraised their work and said, 'Yes, I guess that will have to do.'

Glen walked towards the ladder.

'No, wait! We should finish properly, with a prayer of dedication.'

'How does it go? Is it long?'

She touched his arm. 'I'll say it, but when I look at you, repeat the last line with me.'

The night grew colder. Up in the ten-thousand-foot-high flies of the children's huge stage a new scenery drop was being lowered, contrary to their direction.

Lex looked at her signs and statues – painted and placed on the tree limbs, or on the fort's boards, they looked as incongruous without the cave as living-room furniture set out on a lawn. She recited, 'Hills, bays, streams, marshes, near land, far land, be good to us; keep us from all injury and from death; take away from us every pain, every ill; bring us safely home.'

She looked at Glen and they repeated together, 'Bring us safely home.'

*

The scores of gulls roosting on the sandbar were the first to know the weather would break. They woke as the air changed and began making a sleepy, creaking complaint. Minutes later the first strokes of rain scored dark lines through the dust on leaves.

Jerome Bradley's gentle-tempered ram, billeted most of the summer away from the rigour of steep hills and ewes, looked up as the girl limped past him, her jacket held up over her head. Another female child out walking at an odd hour of the night. The drops on his oily wool remained distinct and dome-shaped for some time.

It rained harder. The heat, which for weeks had filled every unsealed space in every house, which had lain down in the deep grass without flattening the deep grass, was suddenly under assault, its leisurely strength disturbed, shredded and washed away.

The dried blood on the nail prised from a split board and dropped by the woodshed turned to liquid again. The three-petalled flowers, painted in powder on the platform of the tree fort, were quickly erased by the rain. And the statues, a second generation of idols, melted and bled from the wet branches.

From their sunken drum shanties, eels rose to feed – morays not congers. And the plum tree with red-skinned, yellow-fleshed fruit, leaning over the Keenes' boundary fence, began to take in water, which would soon make the ripe plums swell and split their skins – growing sores for the wasps to kiss when the weather cleared.

TAWA

1

Steph was asleep in the bed that crossed the foot of Lex's like – if you were to draw a diagram – the horizontal above the first vertical in Hangman, representing the gallows. Lex listened to her sister's settled steady breathing and thought of how, only a year before, she had cured Steph of her thumb-sucking. Sleep deprivation – that's how Lex had done it. She had listened for the click at the end of each suck, the rhythm of a tongue breaking its seal between thumb and palate. 'Wake up!' Lex would shout. 'Get your thumb out of your mouth!' As long as she clicked, Steph wasn't allowed to sleep. Steph had given up thumb-sucking, and also chewing on the neck of her pyjamas, which produced a more subtle and loose slurp and was far more difficult to police – but Lex was dedicated and managed.

It was one thing to intervene between a nine-year-old and the habit of a lifetime – all *that* required was vigilance, persistence, flintiness, qualities Lex had in abundance. *This* was a more difficult problem. It wasn't a habit Steph had, but a compulsion – and *it* had *her*. How to separate them, soil and roots, tumour and organ? How to uproot, excise, exorcise?

Lex's heart went off like a gun battery. She sat straight up to get her head away from the pillow and resonating bedsprings. Her blood pushed like a flood through a sump in an underground river. Her lamp went out; she turned over and over in the dark.

The old man was *inside* her little sister. His crooked fingers, his stink, his reasonableness – 'That's enough for today, dear, we don't want to make your little pussy sore.' His horrible husbandry.

After a moment the darkness cleared, came apart in clots, like carrion birds startled from their perch on a corpse. On Lex's sheets, beneath her hands, were handprints in sweat. Steph was still peacefully asleep, but other gentle noises in the room had ceased and Lex was being listened for, as if she were dangerous. She said, 'Tish, Buster,' and heard the noises resume. A mouse footed it up a wire ladder; tissue paper tore and rustled as another mouse began housekeeping the nest. A sunflower seed cracked and its husk dropped.

Lex lay down. And, instead of thinking about the situation, she began to consider the man.

A friendly neighbour, he'd encouraged the girls' parents to call him Crit, a short form of his surname. There was an empty section between their properties, where the downhill neighbours, whose house fronted onto Oak Avenue, grazed their pet lamb. From the Keenes' back windows you could look across the cropped grass to Mr Critchlow's fence and his orchard on the slope – an orchard of apple, quince and plum trees. Crit's plums would ripen before the Keenes' and he would turn up at their back door carrying a canvas bucket by its rope handle, the bucket filled with plums of red skin and yellow flesh. Crit always smiled, and although he was short, he would still tilt his head deferentially down when he talked to Frank Keene. His eyes turned up as a child's do in wary admiration of some adult.

Had her parents ever *said* anything about Critchlow? Lex did recall advice she'd filed away, acted on, forgotten to repeat to anyone. '*Don't go in his house.*' Which of them had said that – Hester or Frank? One spoke, the other nodded, neither looked. Lex could see their eyelids – that was her memory, no meaningful looks, but the maze of veins in their adult eyelids.

Lex was retentive of what she'd witnessed. She could replay what she'd seen and hadn't understood, until she did understand it. For instance, there had been a scene at Critchlow's gate.

It was late summer, the Keene family's first Paremata summer, when the girls discovered the old soldier neighbour with his door always open. Crit's house was enticing, a twenties beach cottage built to the right scale for its windowbox geraniums and the blue budgie hung up to air by the open door. Crit kept a stock of homemade iceblocks, blunt cones of frozen cordial from which it was fun to suck the syrup that never set as hard as plain water, but remained fluent, honey in a honeycomb of white ice. He let Lex and Steph ride back and forth standing on the bottom bar of his gate; never said, 'Mind the hinges.'

Early in that first April the father of the two girls across the road came to have a word with Frank. They went into the kitchen and closed the door. Jo made a move to turn down the television, but Steph was glued to *Secret Squirrel* and the men remained inaudible, even through an ineffectual screen of wood veneer over hollow panels. That evening, or maybe the one following, Lex edged up the steps from Bayview Road, one at a time, backwards and on her bottom. She was following her father, who had gone out to look at and listen to the altercation at Critchlow's gate. Lex saw Critchlow stooped and submissive before three fathers of the neighbourhood, and one young constable. Frank Keene seemed uncharacteristically distressed and edgy. He'd come to a standstill between his gate and Critchlow's, and stood side on, as though he was about to retreat. Mr Dunn suddenly took Crit by his shirt-front and began to shake him. Critchlow put his hands up to shield his head and the young constable interposed himself. 'Sir, please!' he said, with indignant emphasis. 'He's an old man.'

Maybe someone looked Lex's way then, or perhaps her father had turned and was starting back down the road, for Lex ducked and ran down the boxed earth steps, careful to find the raised board edges under the joints of her toes. Her left hand hit the smooth patch where everyone touched the branch that overhung the path, touched and ducked down. Lex had spied but not understood. She sealed the scene away to replay it four years later when she'd set herself to think about the man instead of the situation. She replayed it and believed she understood. Then she remembered more, things she'd heard, fertile kernels of information – for remembering was like watching bulbs appear from dry soil in a shaken garden sieve.

Lex and Jo once sat above the road, opposite Critchlow's gate, behind a screen of young pohutukawa. The Dunn girls were with them, cross-legged on the gritty ground, legs hidden in the bells of their skirts. Though the younger girl was silent, she was the subject of the older girl's talk. Crit had *fiddled* with her. 'He got her to take her panties off. Daddy says Mr Critchlow is old and has gone a little funny. Funny in the head. He's *sunk* to interfering with young girls. That's what Daddy said.' Jo turned to her sister to check. 'Do you know what she means?' Lex nodded. She knew Jo would explain further, knew 'interfering' was sex. Mr Dunn had implied that, because Mr Critchlow was old and incapacitated, he was like a toothless lion. No longer one of the 'higher predators', Critchlow was on a reduced diet of the easy, the unsatisfactory – young girls – for lack of anything better.

Lex's thoughts banked, came around for another pass at the past. She saw the kitchen door was *open*, and Mr Dunn was talking to her father about joining the Paremata Residents' Association. Then Lex remembered Hester, not warning, but merely saying of Critchlow, 'Don't bother him, girls. Don't go in his house. If he asks you in just *decline politely*.'

Lex replayed her memories, and believed that she was finally able to understand their content. For years she had known that Critchlow was dangerous. She had been warned, but wasn't sure *who* had warned her.

Four years ago Steph was almost always at Hester's side, an unweaned calf, never in danger. Nothing had come of the scene at Critchlow's gate. Perhaps the police had decided that this time a warning would serve – Critchlow had only forgotten himself, and would behave. Lex and Jo never told their younger sister the little they'd learned. They weren't in the habit of sharing with her what they knew. Steph had too often shown a confused sense of loyalty, was a tell-tale, didn't know whose side she was on in the old war of resistance between children and adults. It was a habit they had – keeping Steph in the dark.

In the dark, in her stew of bedding come adrift, Lex listened to her sister inhale and exhale, cleanly, without childish impediments. But in Lex's mouth was a promise, pushing down on her tongue. She couldn't tell. Why couldn't she tell? Because Steph said, 'Mummy will ask me why I keep on going there.' Lex *knew* why and so she couldn't repeat Steph's guess at their mother's question as a question of her own: 'So, why do you?' Lex knew, and she wouldn't share what she knew, wouldn't even throw a line to her little sister: 'I think you go because . . .' Because any line Lex could throw was anchored to her own secret.

Awake after midnight in the hours she was to know thoroughly in the future, frozen, deciding, dividing herself over and over, unsharing, Lex asked herself not, 'What am I going to do?' but a more compromising question, 'Should I be doing what I am doing?'

2

It was the day of the Tabloid Sports, compulsory 'fun'
alternative to the athletics eliminations which, at the end
of the term, led on to interschool sports, the Wellington
Regional Secondary School Athletics. Athletics weren't
compulsory. Not everyone was good at them and, unlike
other things that not everyone was good at, there was no
final measurable benefit to the 'world outside the school'
as there was with qualifications and grades. What was
'compulsory' in the Tabloids was *taking part*, if only in the
juvenile spectacle of hot potato races, or gumboot throws.
The upper forms were exempt from everything but reporting
on time to the grassy bank between the motorway and
playing fields. They had to attend, but didn't have to watch,

and so the slouches, grouches and nonconformists sat way up in the shade of the conifer hedge and performed.

When Lex saw her sister Jo and Jo's set of Sixths whose form teacher was the school's music and drama man, she imagined performances. They were clowning around, some would say, but it was a hard kind of play, a play with codes about who they wanted to be. One womanly girl ran a grass stalk across the sulky mouth of a big hairy boy and, no matter what else they were doing, every other member of the set watched. Another girl was doing a Kiwi accent to mimic her police cadet boyfriend, and they all smiled. Because she was good at it, the girl had kept the game up longer than everyone else. But Lex knew they smiled not just at this girl's wit, but because Jo's friend Ian had first started the Kiwi accent game in *imitation* of this girl, who didn't know she was now producing an exaggerated version of herself, as she explained that she'd just put a 'plum runse' through her hair, speaking with a rising inflection, as if to ask *had she*, while saying she had. Her buddy, an opaque Greek girl, was laughing with malicious appreciation. Another boy, whose drawings from life were more lifelike than anyone else's, was pulling up his socks, again. Beside him lounged a girl who had been born with a harelip and who, two-thirds of the way through twenty years of correct-ive operations, had a swollen arch to her top lip like a skewed cupid's bow, spoke with a lisp, always looked sceptical, and was very attractive. This girl was the womanly one's buddy, as Life-drawing, the fussy cherub, was Ian's. The Sixths were in a pack now, but had come to the pack, for the most part, in same-sex pairs. The lower forms were full of pairs, as if the whole school had spent its childhood learning how to mate, to form exclusive alliances. In Jo's group the alliances were changing, the general trend being that same-sex couples split to form new pairings of girl and boy, with, since these were nonconformists, a certain measure of resistance.

Jo *wouldn't* be Life-drawing's girlfriend, although he'd shown interest by groping her at a party. Jo had declared preferences, as though she'd already imagined a man for herself, someone dark, hairy, older, hearty and *fertile* – for they'd have ten children – a man whose eyebrows met.

Ian was a homosexual and, because he was also an exhibitionist, he'd tell anyone – except his family and teachers. Though some of the teachers were given opportunities to guess. At a school cabaret, Ian had had the Deputy Head out in the hall foyer with a torch looking for his mother's pearls, which had poured from their broken string. Ian had been having vapours. The Deputy Head, however, didn't himself act vapid, pretend it was all pretence, but seemed amused, protective, exasperated, as though he knew – knew and didn't mind. Jo's group deduced an attitude from this anecdote and thereafter held the Deputy Head in high regard, and would be respectful and co-operative only for him, and for the music teacher – who was *almost* one of them. Would be, except that, when they visited his flat, they had noticed the unconfiding nudity of his walls, then found the art prints of naked men rolled up and stowed behind his couch. If only he hadn't *hidden* from them he'd be one of them.

Of Jo's group, Ian had the most trouble escaping the gravity of his family, who lived in an ex-State house on the flats of Tawa. Ian was the eldest of four brothers. His parents

171

couldn't afford to spring for the long pants and blazer that, as a Sixth, he was now allowed to wear. His friends had them, and looked more boys' school than schoolboy. Ian wore the grey shirt and shorts of the junior school, but compensated by removing the handle from his satchel so he had to carry it nursed before him, a practice mandatory for girls. In Lex's class only the maths whizz carried her bag by its handle.

Outside school hours they led their real lives. Their invisible real lives. For even at their leisure these kids were poor and inconsiderable, perpetually pupils, in training for citizenship. In 1973 there were no shops especially for teens – unless you counted the juvenile section of children's wear in Kirkcaldies or the DIC, mainly devoted to the sale of school uniforms by priestly shop assistants who preserved the sanctity of the fitting room by speaking only to the parents of the bodies being fitted.

'Outside school hours' Ian caught the train to Paremata and the Keenes' house, where he lay on the living-room floor listening to Frank's Tchaikovsky. Ian flattered Jo with his own version of her father's programme of musical appreciation. Ian's programme was more concerned with the lives of the great. The story of how a despairing Tchaikovsky deliberately drank water tainted by cholera. Or – Ian held up one finger to show Jo she must hush and listen to Mahler's French horns mournfully representing a father calling through the hills for his dead infant daughters.

Lex would watch Ian hold forth, astonished that Jo tolerated his lectures. Jo now had no time for Frank's attempts to expand her officially gifted mind. She refused to listen to Bach or to read Proust. Yet, for Ian, she would keep her silence through *Sleeping Beauty* and *The Song of the Earth* in order to charm out his confidences, the bewitching dilemma he faced of *how to be who and what he was.*

Lex watched Jo's friends on the day of the Tabloid Sports, camped in the shade at the very top of the grassy bank, and saw power – the united power of their difference. These were not oddballs, like her friend Stella. These young people were proficient, they were the kids who populated the school plays and whose talent and energy earned those productions reviews in the city dailies. They weren't as independently unassailable as the other stars of the school – the yachties Barnes and Jones, Mexted of the First Fifteen – but together these kids were an entity with prickles, blossoms, and nectar. *What end to pick it up by?*

Lex reached the head of the line. 'Isabel Keene,' her form teacher said. Goldman had mistranscribed her name onto his roll on the first day of school and subsequently reproduced his mistake by photostat, and every time he called on her. 'Is a bell necessary on a bike?' he would say, then think her slow or humourless when she just frowned at him.

Goldman said, 'You have to volunteer for four activities on the circuit.' He presented the list. Lex would be required to show four stamps at the end of the afternoon to be signed off as a participant.

'In what way is this fun?' Lex asked him, and he replied that it wouldn't do her any harm.

He mustn't get her wrong; she didn't mind joining in, it was just that if there were requirements then it *was* compulsory – 'compulsory' implied force – and since when was 'forced' fun? No, she wasn't planning to be a lawyer – she'd make a better beachcomber, she said, perhaps having misconstrued the 'drop-out' fad for futures in beach-bumming. Or she'd be a spy like OPSTUV and QRSTUW, whose names her friend Stella had stencilled on her forearm. She showed him the thick tattoos in blue biro, and added, 'You know them. They're cronies of Qwerty.'

Goldman told Isabel not to be so silly and sulky. If she wouldn't take an interest he'd sign her up for the *real* events. Lex decided to cut her losses, dodge the hurdles and sprints, and the long-distance race her friend Stella liked because it took her out of school grounds. (And, since nothing was expected of Stella, no one would complain when she dawdled in at home time with her lips dyed by Fru-Ju, or glossed by Jelly-Tip.)

Lex put herself down for the high jump and long jump. 'I can do that,' she said, and her voice caught like a poorly oiled hinge. Her words came out in the same odd warbling squeak they had had when, during an interrogation conducted by her science and form teachers and in front of the headmaster, she'd been asked how, since she'd got either C minus or D all year on her exercises in science, she'd managed to come top of the class in the end-of-year test? She told them that she had learned the textbook. She seemed to be telling the truth for, when they posed quest-ions, she looked down as though reading then described diagrams and reproduced textbook language in a digested form – memorised, comprehended, repackaged. Then she'd added, 'It turned out it was interesting,' as though chiding them for hiding something from her all year.

'Go jump then.' Her teacher was irritated. Goldman

knew Lex was unreliable. He thought she should be treated firmly, for she was lazy and insolent, or gently, for she was timid and gloomy – but it was impossible to do *both*. The fact was, Goldman would be happier in an all-boys' school. He didn't like romping or slovenly girls, goody-good girls, sly and mocking girls, or clammily shy girls. But here he was in Tawa, required to teach – that is, to take occasional notice of – all these girls, each one in some way a dissenter.

With Lex dismissed, Goldman faced Stella. Stella was a chubby, mottled English girl Lex had consented to be friends with, and who had, in the course of the year, put herself so far beyond the pale of school culture she was in a realm of pure style. Stella's shiny congested eyes alarmed even her friends, though they admired her other creepy accoutrements: her one black glove and the stainless steel jewellery she wore and did detention for every day, patiently, like she was paying for the privilege of difference.

'Miss Morrissey,' Mr Goldman said, 'what will it be?' His pen poised over his clipboard. Stella replied with a line from an Alice Cooper song. But, whereas Alice would howl it out, Stella delivered it in a hopeful questioning way. '*I love the dead?*' she said, as she had that morning when asked for her French homework, then again, politely, on receipt of the chicken chips and creaming soda Lex had fetched her from the school canteen, then once more, tenderly, to another friend when asked *are you all right?*

The teacher threatened to choose for her.

'Go ahead, mate, but nothing that puts a strain on me arms,' Stella said, emerging from her game, or her fugue, for the first time that day. Goldman made his notation then pulled orange, green, and yellow dots off the rolls he carried

175

and pressed them onto the shoulder of Stella's Manchester United shirt, as far from her big soft breasts as he was able. Stella said, with gratitude, '*Before they're cold*' – sepulchral, as Alice would, permitting herself to move on to the next line of the song.

Lex could never keep up a game like Stella's. Her friend's self-discipline was formidable, even if, as the school supposed, misapplied.

In Tawa College almost all self-expression was dissent, except that which took place behind a music stand in music lessons, or glistened silently when pegged out to dry in the art room. True to the school's culture, Mr Goldman sneered a little at the girls who swapped posters of Donny Osmond from the back covers of *Pink* or *Foxy*. But the swaps were representative of a shared interest, like discussions of the latest in *The Young and the Restless*, which some girls from houses in near streets – those with lunch passes – caught in the lunch hour. This discussion took place every afternoon in the first minutes of Goldman's own class – Social Studies – the first period following lunch, when 3Go's collective attention was at its most scraggy. Goldman barely tolerated the nonsense of soaps and poster swaps in form meetings, and curled his lip to curb the girls' enthusiasm. He gave Stella detentions because, after all, rules regarding the uniform *were* uniform. But he never considered it tolerance when, in Sixth Form history, the girls kicked their heels for ten minutes while five boys from the First Fifteen, whose coach he was, went over Saturday's game or complained about Mexted's lack of team spirit.

Lex and Stella waited to see what their friends chose. They saw one off, waving, towards the hurdles and, if not glory, at least a decent showing. The friends were four who shared a bench in science, drew cartoons during class, or wrote comic stories in rounds. They snuck looks at one another's class exercises, copied in a chain along the bench. Stella would occasionally complain, 'You girls just shut your traps,' and, attending to the board herself, would attempt the exercise. She was left-handed and her paper was right beside another girl's, who would copy. It was irresistible. The next along again would peek, and interpret, and reproduce Stella's exercise in an even more bitsy way. Lex copied *this* girl, and Lex's exercise, the most degraded version of Stella's average attempt, looked like a smearily franked stamp, its point of origin obscure. Words and figures were missing in a pattern – if the teacher marking it was *looking* for a pattern – the shape, with some movement sideways, of a hand holding a pen. It was no wonder then that, after her end-of-year test result, Lex was called to judgement by the headmaster, with her form and science teachers appearing as two attorneys, both for the prosecution. The girl next to Lex was questioned too, since she might have noticed something. This girl later said to Lex, 'You know, they still don't believe you. They just think they haven't worked out your trick.' Lex had surprised herself too. Did her test results prove she was clever? Or – rather – what did it mean to be clever? How did it feel? Is this how it felt? This bloated, pecked, pulled-apart, blown-away sensation of the *vividness* of things. Lex had said to her friend, wistfully, 'I wish they'd just called me clever. And, besides, if I *did* have a trick they couldn't discover, wouldn't that make me clever? Well, at least resourceful?'

*

After the gumboot throw Lex and Stella had some blue goo. The Seventh Formers in the refreshment tent said it was their best seller. They had been saying so since they opened, so of course it sold. For ten cents the girls got a waxed cup full of goo, made of sugar, gelatin, and blue food colouring. A taste and a look about told the girls why the goo was so popular. Stella pulled a face. Her mother was into wholefood, and, make no mistake, this was calf not agar. Twenty paces from the tent, kids were up-ending their cups into their hands and throwing jelly. Lex knew Stella couldn't resist and that, as the only Third Former to hand, she was Stella's only possible target. Lex gave Stella her goo and ran off to the high jump.

Miss Sanchez, one of the gym teachers, was supervising the girls' high jump. Neither of Tawa's gym teachers was a New Zealander. Miss Sanchez had graduated from a Californian college. She was exotic, had a Mexican name, but was blonde. Her limbs were hairless and tanned, a tan like a good strong ceramic glaze. Her gym shoes were nothing like the pupils' – by this time of year at best freshly painted with the fruity smelling frosting used in every Kiwi household to whiten canvas footwear. Miss Sanchez's shoes were white leather, highly structured, foot hugging, with a little lift to the heel. With them she wore white cotton foot socks with small red bobbles at the ankle to prevent them from being trodden down into the shoes no matter how vigorously she stepped out.

Lex reported to Miss Sanchez, took a deep breath and plunged into the deodorised zone of the gym teacher's body. 'I jump from the left,' Lex said.

'Yes? Well, get over there then, and watch Kim and

178

Karen do the Fosbury Flop.'

That was easy, Lex thought. Miss Sanchez didn't know her, hadn't sorted her out yet, neither a pleasure to teach like Kim and Karen, sinewy Fifth Formers, nor a slow performer like Jo, whose co-ordination was so poor that the other gym teacher, Mr Speikman – Dutch by way of Indonesia, and apt to spice up health classes with horror stories about sun stroke or tropical parasites – took Hester and Frank Keene aside at a parent-teacher evening to ask about Jo's middle ear. As a Sixth Former Jo was exempt now from gym, but, in Lex's circle, there was always Stella, who couldn't keep her chin above the parallel bar for more than a second. Lex was just one of the crowd – even now, in the short line, the line to the left.

Lex was right-handed but always jumped from the left. In her last year of primary school, at the start of the summer sports season, when the grass was tender but finally dry underfoot, the Form Twos were lined up before the notched poles of the high jump and divided into two groups. Six or so southpaws to the left of the jump, and the rest right. They began an uneven alternation – three from the line to the right would take a turn, followed by one from the left. The bar was one of those steel reinforcing rods usually seen sprouting from the foundations of new buildings. Lex bumbled through the bar even on its lowest notch. Something was wrong. She had thought she'd be good at this. She began to imagine Sports Day and Steph doing what *she* always had – not watching her sister, looking away unconcerned by the results of any race in which Jo ran. For Jo always came in last. Jo wouldn't show distress, if she

even felt it. She would only complain, reasonable, a peti-
tioner to each teacher in every year that, since it was clear
she was slow and wouldn't improve, why did she have to
compete? 'It's important that you take part,' they would
reply, and Jo would take the *same* part in all four of her
primary schools and in every year, the part of the slowest
and clumsiest child in school.

'Keene, you've got two left feet,' Lex's teacher said, and
called the class away to line up, in a kink-backed snake,
before the runway to the long jump. At the back of the
line Lex practised nonchalance, until, 'Would Miss Keene
like to take her turn?' the teacher asked in tones of, 'Is
Miss Davis ready for her close-up?'

Lex ran along the runway, and knew it would be all
right even as she was running. She made a small skip to
select which foot would hit the mark, hit it, took off, thrust
her legs before her and struck a patch of dry sawdust beyond
the churned damp place where the tallest children had
made their landing.

'Her feet didn't hit the mark, Sir!' said one of the basket-
ball girls. But the adjudicator disagreed.

The following day Lex asked if she could approach the
high jump from the left. She had to argue about it, since
right-handed people were almost invariably right-footed
too. But the teacher had nothing to lose and let her, and
Lex went over each notch, surviving all eliminations, until
the class was standing around waiting for the height that
would knock her out, the slight girl who seemed to hang in
the air at the apex of each jump, as though her body was
considering whether or not to come down at all.

*

'I hope I won't disgrace myself,' Lex said to the person beside her. 'I used to be good at this.'

She knew she was still good. A month before, on the first hot day in October, she had persuaded Steph to hold one end of a bamboo stake, and had threaded the other end through a loop-headed steel stanchion she poked into the lawn. She practised. Her mother came down from the house with a bucket of scraps for the compost. Hester stood watching for a while, plugging and unplugging her mouth with her cigarette, making that raspy 'phip' Lex liked to hear, since it was a sure sign of her mother's nearness, whether Hester could be seen or not. When Lex was half-asleep, for instance, and her mother passed their open bedroom door, she could hear Hester's soft footsteps then the more succinct 'phip' of a snapped cord of smoke. Hester watched Lex jump, then went to find a saw to remove the small branch of the walnut that Lex kept having to duck, bent double to sail between bar and branch. Hester cut the branch off, cauterised the cut with waxy brown tar and left them to practise.

Steph got bored holding up her end of the bamboo, but she was under Lex's eye, out of trouble, and if Lex went off to pee then came back to find the bamboo tilted down at one end –

'Are you all right?' The girl beside Lex had an arm across her stooped back.

Then Miss Sanchez arrived. 'You're hyperventilating; you're curling up because you're hyperventilating.' The teacher cast about for a paper bag. Lex breathed into someone's brown paper lunch bag until she uncurled, could smell raisins and oranges, and had hunted *it* into a dark corner of her head, her thoughts about that undefendable, indefensible person, her younger sister, who was home from school each weekday a whole hour before she was.

'What was all that about?' the gym teacher asked.

'I don't know. Maybe I breathed in a bug.'

'So – that was choking?' Miss Sanchez was dubious. She signalled for the high jumping to resume, but stayed beside Lex. 'Watch Kim,' she said.

Kim was a tall freckled Maori, a figure of bone articulated by sinew and long regular muscles. Kim ran, curving into the jump, and went over the bar shoulders first, flexed her spine and kicked up her legs, in a wonderful mixture of control and abandon.

'A boy at my primary school who spent a year in America came back trying to do that, but we only had sawdust on the other side of the jump and so they stopped him.'

'Just as well. He could have injured his neck.'

'I can only do a scissors jump.'

'Are you fit to try?'

Lex said she was fine and was allowed to take her turn. She went over, bounded off the sliding pile of foam squabs. She could do this all afternoon.

Girls were eliminated and Lex got to jump more often, until there were just three of them before the jump – the others having been released to go on around the circuit. Kim and Karen, the two tall Fifth Formers, stood before their coach – for they were both in the athletics team, and had been encouraged to call Miss Sanchez 'coach'. They were bent over, blowing, hands gripping their legs above their knees. Lex was pink but still breathing easily. 'I guess you must be fit too,' Miss Sanchez said. She sounded resentful, as though Lex had been lying to her.

'I go out canoeing with a friend,' Lex explained. 'Can I have a look at this jump?'

The gym teacher nodded, and Lex went up to stand under the bar, which brushed the top of her curls. She came back. 'I don't think I can jump that, but the ground is much better here than the lawn at home.'

The Fifth Formers looked at her with interest. 'So, you practise?' one said.

Lex's face lit up. 'I love jumping.'

Kim said, 'I'm eight-and-a-half stone, how much do you weigh?'

'I don't know. I was four-and-a-half after my bronchitis, but Dad buys me stout and I have half a pint a night, for the iron, and he's fattening me up.'

'Stout?' Miss Sanchez was baffled.

Kim said, 'Like Guinness, Miss Sanchez.' Then, to Lex, 'That's very old-fashioned. Do you get pissed?'

'Yes.'

'Nice side-effect,' Kim said, then looked at the jump. 'Go on, try it.'

Lex walked out wide, eyed the striped bar, knew it would hurt more than her bamboo stake if it clipped her toe. The air below the bar was a barrier, like a sheet of glass. She ran at it, took off, felt nothing at all, or imagined she felt something warm brush her anklebone. She landed at the very edge of the crashpad and staggered off. When she looked back over her shoulder the bar was there, and *still*, as though she'd quietly sauntered under it.

Karen and Kim were talking to Miss Sanchez. 'She's

not getting underneath the jump then going straight up. She takes off miles from it and moves in a curve – '

'Like a ballet dancer.'

'She almost missed the mats, Miss Sanchez. She went *woo-hoo-hoo!* like the Flying Nun.'

The teacher asked Lex whether she'd like to join the athletics team. Lex said no – then – could she think about it?

'It's only two weeks until the Meet. That's six athletics practices, four after school, and one on each Saturday. It's not a big commitment.'

'She shouldn't even have to come to Practice. We could just take her to the Meet and she could do her scissors jump and put the wind up them,' Kim said, with relish.

'Don't you want to learn how to jump? Properly. The way it's done now,' the gym teacher asked Lex. 'Of course you do. And if you're in the team you must come to Practice. Those are the rules. The *commitment* is as important as your performance. More important.'

Lex said yes, all right, she'd do it. A Keene at the interschool sports. Imagine. And what else did she have to do?

3

Lex ran for the early train. She jogged out of D Block and down the slippery, balding bank from the school grounds. There were others running with her – all the northbound pupils keen to get home. As she crossed the second intersection beyond the school, the bells on the level crossing began to ring. She put on a burst of speed and watched the ambling herd ahead of her change character as train friends waved to local friends and took off, to run weaving towards the ramp up over the rail line.

Lex saw Jo walking beside Ian. She touched her sister's arm as she passed and ran sideways a few steps to encourage Jo to follow her.

'Go on,' Ian said to Jo. 'You shouldn't have to listen to

me *going on.*' He was flushed. He looked pleased with himself.

Jo waved to Ian and joined Lex. They avoided the ramp and ran to the fence beside the tracks, climbed over it and waited near the embankment as the train rattled past. Then they crossed the tracks and waded through the piled, rust-coated stones up onto the platform.

The Keene girls were the last on. As the train moved off they stood in the doorwell and caught their breath. Jo had things to tell. She told Lex that Ian was having an affair. Jo said Ian had, (a) Let her in on it, (b) Asked her advice. Jo actually said 'a' and 'b'.

'The guy is another local boy, an eighteen-year-old, who left school last year and works as a builder's apprentice. I think he and Ian live on the same street.' Jo lowered her voice, leaned forward. She was about to offer evidence that Ian wasn't exaggerating, extrapolating from flirtation, a touch, even a kiss. 'Ian says that men are so different – from each other. This guy's spunk is thick, like porridge. This is a bit . . .' Jo pulled a face. She was repeating Ian's boasts as a kind of anecdotal science. This knowledge was priceless, more useful than osmosis or the Krebs Cycle. Ian said that, when he came, he hosed the wall above the bed's headboard. Lex imagined a single bed in a boy's bedroom, the bedroom of this other boy, this *man*, a poster of Deep Purple on the wall perhaps. Jo repeated Ian's description of his hurried efforts to wash spunk, baked hard by body heat, out of his eyebrows before going home to face his mother.

Jo sighed. 'You would think it would be harder for him to get sexual experience than me.' Jo was thinking of homosexuals as a statistical sample. How had Ian acquired something so *rare* when she was surrounded by unavailable heterosexual men? Then again, Jo reasoned, didn't they say that men always had more of an eye out for opportunities? She supposed that two men, each with an eye out, would be more likely to . . .

'The problem with the affair is,' Jo said, 'that this guy comes from a strict Catholic family and he's *consumed by guilt*. He's started calling Ian at odd hours of the night. Drunk. Ian has to rush to pick up the phone before his Mum does.'

Lex just listened. It was an education, or it was gossip, or it was life at one remove. She wondered whether Ian was only worried that he'd be found out, or if he was troubled about how this man must feel – to go, at eighteen, from bed to the bottle, to the phone, to standing – as Jo described – outside Ian's window in the early hours, hidden from the neighbours by a big, leggy Safari Sunset. Luckily, the neighbours' dog was indoors. It had its hip in plaster. The plaster came off next week.

Ian's secret, Jo said, was like an unexploded bomb. 'Always counting down. Every time he stops the clock it starts again.'

The Keene girls got off at Paremata and walked in the heat across the clay wasteland where, two years before, big Ministry of Works earthmoving machines had razed a small hill to make an approach for the proposed motorway extension. The graded land terminated in a steep bank that sloped down above a buried beach into deep water. These earthworks were like a pile of gunpowder still separated by several miles from the grey fuse of motorway. If they ever came together it would all be over; the explosion a germination. The ramp would put forth its four lanes across the channel – not a bridge but a causeway with drains alone to let the tides in and out. The Minister had a vision: twenty-five minutes by car from Plimmerton to Wellington Airport. The protesters had another vision: of young flounder in pale layers, decayed, in a soup of silt.

Jo was complaining now, not of Ian's confidences but of his boasting. 'He asked was it true that it could take a woman, masturbating, twenty minutes to reach orgasm. He said, "How do you stand it?" Apparently it only takes him sixty seconds. But what's so good about that?' Jo peered at her sister – she knew that Lex was *in the know* and should have an opinion.

'Isn't this just more one-upmanship? What's the difference between him saying that, and how he never listens to you talk about the books you've read because they aren't cultural? He's just saying that he's more sensitive than you are, that he's got a hair-trigger. What's the difference between that and crying over Tchaikovsky?'

'I wish you and Ian would bother to talk to each other,' Jo said, mournfully. 'You're such snobs.'

'He's *your* friend.' Lex waved an arm in the direction of the smooth hills on the far side of the harbour. 'Your friends are all miles away from me, way over there with their breasts and beards and blazers and long pants. And I'm *not* a snob.'

'How come you mooch about with a scowl on your face whenever Ian comes over?'

'I'm listening.'

Jo had already reported to Lex her Greek friend's remark about Lex's 'sour face'. Lex had sat herself in front of the mirror and taken a long critical look until she could see, in

188

meeting her own eyes, the look that said, 'Go away', even to herself.

Jo muttered, '*Relief*, as he puts it, in sixty seconds flat. Sounds like an ad for painkillers.'

'Let's walk faster,' Lex said. 'I want to get home.'

4

At five, Lex and her friend Grace were out on the water. They rested with their paddles tucked in the hollow under their ribs, one blade dipped and the canoe turning slowly head-on to the breeze. The girls were beyond the Point between Brown's Bay and Ivey's Bay, in the smooth blue water of the channel near the wedge of a sandbar. The tide was coming in, the water perhaps two feet deep over the sandbar's humpback.

The canoe was still quite new – or new to Grace's family. It was homemade, had a timber frame with canvas tacked to it and was painted with high-gloss house paint. The girls took care where they put their feet, against the frame, not the permeable canvas hide.

It was four years since Grace's father had been on sabbatical in Canada. The family went with him, and came home with a working knowledge of ice hockey and kayaking. But it was several years before Dr Hutton's intermittent want-to-buy ads turned up trumps. Kayaks hadn't yet caught on in New Zealand. Too heavy, perhaps, and not as durable as a dinghy, whose upturned weathered timber or spruce aluminium shells were to be found in every cove or beach on both coasts of the country. The Huttons' canoe was the only one afloat in Paremata Harbour. Other kids had their P-class yachts and the romance of tacking or jibing, the cold drama of canning – Grace, her sisters and brothers had their canoe. It was like an expression of their family rigour – a thin, unpropelled boat for the thin, tight-lipped Huttons.

When the Huttons got their canoe at the end of the previous summer, Grace, a middle child of five, had stood in the shallows waiting her turn. But the other Huttons got bored with canoeing. The younger two began to ask only for a tow on their lilos. The oldest boy got tired of trying to catch Grace and her friend Lex who, after great shows of patience, posted whole hours knee deep in warm Brown's Bay water, would often abscond with the canoe for hours at a time and could be spotted only with the aid of binoculars, paddling in a leisurely voyaging way towards the harbour's far shore. Now, only Grace and Lex ever took the canoe out.

They never wore life-jackets. Life-jackets were rare even among the gaggle of kids in P-class yachts.

In their canoe, Lex and Grace synchronised. Whoever was in the front called out directions, 'Right, one, two, three' – a turn always at half-time of the rhythm of forward progress. They would back at half-time, and sometimes changed direction quickly, and on one order, water banked up against the blades of the braking paddles and the canoe in a slewing turn. If another Hutton did come after them wanting his turn, they always seemed to see the threat simultaneously and switched to doubletime. Whoever led, they were *at one*, their thin browned and muscled arms moving together. The greatest part of their pleasure was this synchronicity.

When the winter came the girls stopped taking the canoe out. All winter it lay on the Huttons' front lawn, and its painted hide darkened with mildew. The girls turned thirteen and got their periods. Then, at Labour Weekend, the sun shone long enough for the canoe to dry out. It was again light enough for the two girls to carry across Paremata Road to the beach at Brown's Bay, into the shallows, then, on the count of three, heave over into the water. Once they were in the canoe and off they synchronised straight away and had only to build up their stamina.

Now that they had no competition – for they came and went quietly – canoeing was just something they'd settled on to do, something which soothed them, something strenuous and disciplined. And when they were out in the middle of the harbour they could talk without being overheard, with no danger of anyone suddenly breaking in on them, yet not face to face, so there was always a protective distance – coupled with the pleasure of suspense, of guessing each other's thoughts. An extension of the sympathy they'd developed to steer their canoe, the *guessing* was another discipline, something else they understood they had to master, an adult skill that might be useful to them.

Now broadside to the breeze, the canoe drifted along the channel. Lex looked up the harbour. They were clear of the shallow headlands along towards Pauatahanui, and Lex could see a khaki smoke of rushes, the wetland bird sanctuary, and the white-painted structure of the bridge over the Pauatahanui Stream.

Grace said, 'What did you do about Steph?'

Lex eyed her friend's back, the drops on Grace's skin where the wind had blown splashes from the working paddles. Lex said she had written Critchlow a letter, which she could show Grace if Grace wanted, because she'd *drafted* it first. That was something she had never done before, even in composing constipated thank-you notes to her South Island grandmother. 'Thank you for the hankies, hairclasp, carnation bath powder . . .'

'It's a sort of warning letter,' Lex said. 'You should come up tomorrow morning and have a look.'

Grace went to Mana College, not Tawa, and, while Lex ran for the early train, Grace made no great effort to get to the station. In fact, Lex often saw Grace from the train window, nearing the bus shelter on the city side of Porirua station, scuffing her feet, her head down to avoid temptation, the sight of a friend waving from the train.

Grace dipped a paddle to turn them into the wind. She asked, 'How much has Steph told you?'

'Not much. She won't tell Mum, because Mum told us not to go in his house.' Lex's tone was uncertain, and her face creased behind her friend's back. 'Actually, I think

Mum told us not to *bother* him.'

Grace said she understood why Steph was scared. Then she was silent and Lex was left looking at her friend's gooseflesh, like a very complex game of join-the-dots that came and went with each gust of wind. After a moment Grace said, formally, as though she'd not simply modified her thought but her *self* before she spoke, 'I understand Steph's reluctance. Sometimes it's impossible to explain things to adults. Adults think they're saying, "I'll help you if I can understand you, if you can make yourself understood" – as if they're coaxing a tongue-tied toddler. But *really* they're saying, "I'll help you if you can put things my way, fit what *you* feel into what *I* already know." So that every time you have to ask for help you end up feeling even less like yourself.'

This was Lex's experience only with teachers, who were an exclusive class of adult. In her last year at primary school her teacher sent her to the headmaster because she wouldn't do her maths. The headmaster sat her down and told her how he wanted to get to the bottom of it – her problem with maths. He was going to ask her why she wouldn't do it, and he didn't want to hear her say that she didn't like it. She was a mature girl. He'd ask her in a mature way. On and on he talked, coaching her to answer in a way that wouldn't irritate him. He flattered and patronised. She kept her eyes on his face, maintained an attentive and respectful expression. Her eyes watered. She was stupefied by his talk. Finally he paused and asked, 'Why won't you do your maths?' And, startled, Lex answered with the truth: she didn't like maths. The headmaster's face went red, he leaned forward, put his hands down on the arms of her chair and boxed her in between its arms and his own. Her insolence was unbelievable, he said. Or was it stupidity? He was very disappointed.

Thinking about this, Lex said to Grace, 'I guess adults expect to be humoured. That's how they treat each other. That's what they're used to.'

'*Would* your mother tell Steph off?'

'Yes. I think so. Also, you know, Critchlow's done it before and he's still around. He doesn't get into trouble.' And Lex told Grace about the Dunn girls and Mr Critchlow's War Record.

'So, he gets another chance every year or so?'

'Something like that.'

The girls noticed then that the canoe had begun to turn in circles, and that the water had become green and choppy. The sun was still out, a bright burr caught in the trees of the Point; but the east, the narrow valley where a metalled road wound away into the Paremata golf course, was stoppered up by a dark cloud. A sneaky easterly was on its way. Easterlies were very rare in Paremata Harbour. Grace and Lex had never been out on the water in an easterly, and they were completely unprepared.

They saw the rain come across the water as the east, the most domestic and sheltered arm of the harbour, blurred. Then the rain was hitting their backs like water from an angled shower head. The canoe went broadside to the wind and tilted. The girls put their paddles down, and the canoe straightened and shot away along the path of the wind. They made for the Point, didn't discuss it, no words were exchanged. Paddling hard and at an angle to the wind they were still driven out, on a trajectory that would take them past the end of the Point, out of Ivey's Bay, and all the way across the harbour towards the far side: Gray's Road, Ken Gray's farm, an empty shore and streams bridged only by wire fences, no road, only sand dunes and strangeness.

Except they wouldn't even get *there*, because rain was filling the canoe.

They began to alternate two strokes right with one left. They never thought to abandon the canoe. When it was almost full, sluggish in the water, they rolled out, slung their arms over its side and pushed their paddles ahead of them through the last few feet of deep water. Then their feet found the rocks at the end of the Point and they hauled the canoe out to wedge it between two boulders.

Lex sat in the cold sea, with rain pouring on her exposed shoulders, and let her sore, shaking arms float. Grace tucked her knees up to her chin to squeeze a stitch out of her side.

'If we'd stayed with the canoe we'd have drowned,' Lex said.

'We *did* stay with the canoe.' Grace corrected her blithely, as though she were a ghost talking to a ghost.

Lex said, 'What I meant to say is, we shouldn't have.'

'Are you kidding? I'd be in such trouble if I lost the canoe.'

They looked at it, swamped, its timber and canvas sodden. They had to empty it out and carry it home. It took nearly ten minutes of rocking the canoe, a little more water slopping out at each rock, until they were able to turn it onto its side, then upside down. Then they carried it home, along the thin, nibbled shore, over the concrete ramps of some boatsheds, the steel rails of others, and under sea-gouged banks. It was hard going and they rested often.

Their exertions kept them warm, or warm at the core, despite the cold rain and wind.

They crossed Paremata Road and set the canoe down on its rack on the Huttons' lawn. Lex said maybe she should run home. She was shivering. Grace told her don't be silly, come in and get dry, borrow some clothes, have a hot drink.

They went through the back door into the kitchen, which smelled of pet food. The dog, very old, its black lips sagging away from its gums, didn't lift its head, but cocked its ears and raised its eyes, and its tail swept the floor. There were air bubbles under the linoleum and the floor crackled as they crossed it. They found towels, wiped the bare skin around their bikinis, which were too insubstantial to remain wet, tiny triangles of nylon joined by shoestring straps. They wrapped their hair in towels and retreated to the Hutton sisters' room.

The bedroom was beside the sunporch, where Dr Hutton had his desk, his reference books and the day bed, neatly made up with army blankets and white sheets folded as flat as the flap on an envelope. Dr Hutton usually slept in this bed. He slept badly – he had been a prisoner of war for several years in some cold barracks in Germany. Lex imagined that Dr Hutton was only ever partly submerged in sleep, that some part of his consciousness always hovered above the place where he had entered, expecting alarms, a rude awakening, blows, bullets that burrowed through darkness, piercing the shelter of his sleep.

There were still three beds in the girls' room. Grace's was in the far corner under her silk sari and her poster of Krishna among the milkmaids. Grace's younger sister's bed was by the door, and heaped with dolls – both her own and

Grace's Barbies, brought back from North America three years ago, and still coveted by other little girls at Paremata School – unique, big-breasted, flexible, their icy blonde hair dreadfully matted now.

The third bed was not made up. It was covered by a crocheted quilt. Above it, on the end of the curtain rail, were a dozen strings of painted clay beads, dust coating their varnish like white mould – the handiwork of the oldest Hutton girl, Justine, who was gone.

Justine Hutton, Jo Keene, and Cathy Brent were always to be seen together – an 'always' of three months' duration when they were all twelve years old. They'd walk home together, Justine already cradling her satchel like a college girl, her head bent, face hidden in her hair. Jo and Justine would talk about their families, about growing up – Jo telling Justine everything. Occasionally one or the other girl would put out a hand to steer Cathy away from the edge of the footpath and the drop through the wattles down to the roofs of the baches at Bottle Creek. Cathy was reading, weaving slowly up the path, on her sealegs, adrift in a book. Justine would save her from the bank; Jo would save her from the curb, like two sheepdogs with one sheep between them.

Five months into that year, Dr Hutton went on sabbatical and took his family with him. They went to Germany, and Justine sent letters about black bread and the Black Forest. They went to Canada and Justine sent letters about 'Eh' and ice hockey. Then she stopped sending letters. The Huttons came home a week before school broke up and all the Hutton kids had new clothes and modified accents – change skin deep. But Justine had *skin*, defenceless, her little nipples poking right through the holes in her crocheted vest, camouflaged among other rough buttons, her varnished clay beads. She had acquired a black leather catsuit, and a blue nylon dress with huge puffed sleeves. All this was remodelling. But Justine talked to Jo, who discovered that her friend was altered inside as well as out. Justine brought Jimi Hendrix and Janis Joplin records to play on the Keene girls' mono record player, for which they had only five disks so far – two greatest hits compilations, *Those Were the Days* and *ChartBusters of '69*, Lex's *Tom Jones Live*, Steph's Joan Baez, and Jo's Mikis Theodorakis. Jo and Justine listened to 'Ball and Chain'. Justine sat crosslegged on the rumpus-room floor and watched – she said – butterflies spinning in a shaft of sunlight. She was tripping. She had a boyfriend, an older man, someone in the neighbourhood. He and she had celebrated Black Mass the other night – she showed Jo photographs of herself, naked, with burning candles on her cupped palms and in the shadowed delta above her thighs. Justine was the first friend Jo had who had turned into a woman. Jo had trouble distinguishing this maturing from other dangerous changes: Justine's waxing breasts from the thickening – it seemed – of the transparent skin over her eyeballs, the light not lost on them, but caught in a thick, bright layer whenever Justine turned to stare.

Jo told Lex that she was worried about her friend. 'She'll get pregnant or . . .' Jo said, then explained the implication of all the other things in the photographs she'd seen: a dagger placed between Justine's breasts – oh – *all of it*, drugs, blood-letting, sex, some perverted married man up Seaview Road . . .

Then Justine went missing.

The police who came to interview Jo said, on their first visit, that they thought Justine had run away. Jo told them everything she could remember, even the less striking information, like the first name of the *other* boyfriend, the Hell's Angel – who, it transpired, had taken Justine to Australia. The police visited the Keenes regularly for a time. They didn't want to simply *ask* Jo whether she'd heard from Justine, but had to make their way to that question by sketchier routes than questions. The uniformed cop would stand beneath Lex's bird mobile, made from twigs, wool, and strips of paper curled between the blades of her scissors. He would blow until the birds rocked and twirled. The detective sat at the dining table and took his time. Frank would see them out, say he *knew* his daughter, they could believe her, she wasn't keeping Justine's secrets – Jo was sad that Justine was gone, she'd like her back too.

Three years later, when Lex was sitting on Justine's bed, under the bunched leis of dusty beads, Justine had not been heard from.

Once her friend was installed, Grace went to boil the jug. Lex stripped Justine's bed, wrapped herself in the crocheted rug. Grace's older brother came and stood in the doorway. He had been in one of Paremata School's composite classes with Lex. He was one of the boys not above talking to the school's lepers – the thief, the kid-with-cooties, the kid-with-a-stammer, the very-quiet-girl. He had been the heavy-hitter in the baseball team Lex captained. Lex had been appointed captain because she was the last picked for a team, the slightest, quietest girl, who then helped her team to victory with her plan for the batting order, and her signals to direct both skilful batting and sly base-stealing. Her team were the champions, and won a woodwork-class planed-and-turned timber shield on which Lex – appointed to decorate it – misspelled her school's name.

Grace's brother wanted to say that he'd seen her in town the other day with glitter on her face and blue food colouring in her hair.

'And my platforms, and my black velvet jacket.'

'And your fat friend.'

She stared at him, her lack of expression more severe than severity.

'So, do you have the latest Bowie?'

Yes, she did, though she still preferred *Ziggy Stardust*.

Grace's brother defended *Aladdin Sane*. Rick Wakeman's piano, he said.

Boys always knew about music. And Lex recalled this boy policing the stereo at primary school socials. Not dancing. Squatting by the stereo in his purple paisley shirt, jeans, buckskins, to drive off others, the boys in jumpers and shirts, or the girls in frocks with cut-away shoulders, even the one lucky girl in the polka-dot maxi apron dress. While he was there no one would *dare* put on 'Knock Three Times on the Ceiling If You Want Me'.

He told Lex that he really wasn't into that glam stuff.

'Neither am I – not Slade or The Sweet or Gary Glitter.' She pulled a face. Gary Glitter – that travesty. 'My friend, my *fat* friend, loves Alice Cooper, but I think they're just a rock opera. I like T. Rex, but don't have much choice about it since the kids at school think I look like Marc Bolan.

For me it's Bowie. He's the one.' It was like she was talking about the Godhead, the Three-in-One.

'He's OK – musically.'

Lex felt tired. Already boys her age were turning into the men who *owned* music, the men in charge of the stereo, who would ask her to listen to this or that and perform the sacramental gesture of positioning the stylus over the track, then pressing the lever that lowered the arm. Experts on technical matters, these boys and men would ask her to hear the difference between an Archiv or Deutsche Grammophon recording of Mahler's Fifth – the performance Bruno Walter conducted in 1939. In the silences the audience could be heard to cough and shuffle their feet. Lex would forget to listen to whatever it was she was supposed to hear, the attack of strings or horns, because she was already gone, dreaming about that audience, those coughing, shuffling people, their circumstances, their refined attentiveness, with the War suspended over them like a great wave – death by suffocation.

Lex said, to fend off this latest expert, 'Yes, the innovations of the music – Mick Ronson playing bass like it's lead – Rick Wakeman's honky-tonk piano.' She spoke as though making a recitation, and she looked over the top of his head.

Grace appeared and edged past him. She gave a steaming cup to Lex and told her brother to push off. Grace asked Lex should she ring tomorrow?

'Just to say when you're coming. You know about our phone.'

The Keenes' phone was making strange clicking noises whenever it was picked up. A little way into a call the phone would settle down, but there were the odd incursions of noise, taps and squeaks like somebody struggling to open a sticky window. Frank Keene had decided the phone was bugged. Frank was a friend of Bill Sutch, he'd been to Bill's house when Dr Sutch was released on bail after being charged under the 1951 Official Secrets Act. Shortly after that, the phone began to misbehave. The telephone repairman was baffled, then a little coy about the peculiarities.

Grace said, 'Dad says Dr Sutch is a traitor. What do you think? Do you think he *did* pass information?'

'Dad thinks not. Dad says it's bloody terrible – Bill Sutch has a "good brain" – Dad likes good brains. He says that Sutch is getting a lousy deal.'

Lex's and Grace's fathers were members of what in any other country might have been termed 'the intelligentsia'. But intellectuals, like snakes, weren't native to New Zealand. Frank was a lefty, had helped hand out food parcels to wharfies' families during the '51 lockout, and had climbed to the top of the radio mast in Titahi Bay in 1961 to interrupt the broadcast of a rugby game with a recording of news about the shootings in Sharpeville. Frank Keene wasn't, like some of his friends, a member of the communist party. Frank had a typically atheist suspicion of *joining*, of signing up for anything.

'I should get home now,' Lex said. 'Steph went to visit her friend up Oak Avenue, but she's due back before tea, like me.'

'You can't stand watch over her.'

'No.' Lex was shivering again, but got up and threw off the crocheted rug. The evening light put a hand in the window and wrapped shadowy claws around her ribcage. She put her wet T-shirt back on, worked the thongs of each jandal between her damp toes, and walked out, creaking.

5

Grace and Lex sat on either end of Lex's bed, their legs folded under them. They had pens and jumbo pads, and between them on the quilt lay a packet of coloured pencils. They had just exchanged drafts. It took half a minute to proof each letter. Lex felt her attention skate out the far side of the document without having entangled itself in 'love' or 'yours faithfully'. She told Grace they should put 'your enemy' at the note's close, and that since Grace's handwriting was more mature than her own, it would be Grace's copy they'd put in Critchlow's box. Critchlow would take Grace's handwriting more *seriously* than Lex's, for how could anyone expect firmness from a hand that formed such spindly mismatched characters?

Critchlow

We know what you are up to and we are watching your every move. You will not get away with what you are doing. You are an evil man who is doomed already. Do not make your situation worse by continuing to do what you have been doing.

Make no mistake

WE CAN SEE YOU

WE CAN HEAR YOU

WE CAN TESTIFY AGAINST YOU

'It's not true though, is it? Neither of us is an eyewitness. And I haven't even heard Steph's testimony.' Grace bent over the hardback atlas she was using as a desktop, opened the coloured pencils and selected a black one. She began to draw a skull at the top of the page – left the appropriate lines broken to accommodate the red and yellow flames she then drew shooting from the skull's eye sockets.

Hester hurried in with a pile of ironed handkerchiefs, which she divided and stowed in the girls' sock and panties drawers. Lex and Grace simultaneously turned their letters face down and looked at Hester who said, amused, 'I'm not interested in what you're doing.' She stopped in the doorway. 'But Lex, you should go out and offer Steph some encouragement, she's very near to breaking that record.'

Lex could hear that Steph was still at it. The strangled squawk of the spring in Steph's pogo stick had been going on for well over an hour. Steph was trying for the *Guinness Book of Records*, the record for continuous pogoing. She was jumping on the asphalt slope of the Keene driveway. It was her last attempt. She was too shy to try it in the school grounds, and none of Paremata's footpaths were wide enough to save her in the event of one of her occasional moments of overbalancing, when she lurched off at an angle, recovered, then went back to her usual small, energy-efficient jumps-in-place. Steph's attempts at the record had left little pits in the asphalt. The drive was due for resurfacing. The truck would come Monday, Frank had been told.

Lex told her mother they'd be along to count off Steph's last hundred. While she could hear the pogo stick, Lex could relax her vigilance. Even the mandatory separation of school hours was becoming difficult for her. She'd been so good – hadn't followed the fun, the trail of Jo's friends as they walked through D Block at lunchtime drawing gay liberation signs in purple crayon. Lex even did some homework to avoid a detention. She hadn't had to *choose* to give up canoeing. Barnes the harbourmaster had seen her and Grace in trouble on the water (and, before he'd launched his own dinghy, had seen them land safely on the Point). But he did ring Dr Hutton. Lex and Grace were under a ban. 'It won't last more than a week,' Grace said. 'Dad will forget. They always forget. The only thing they *never* forget is to remind me to take my pill.'

Did Grace mean the contraceptive pill? Lex had asked. Her friend Stella was on the pill for irregular periods. It must be something like that. Surely Lex would know about it if Grace had a boyfriend.

'My tranquillisers,' Grace had explained. Calmly. 'My parents got tired of me losing my temper. I even slapped Mum once.'

Lex supposed this was the Huttons' reaction to Justine's

delinquency. She couldn't imagine *her* parents taking Jo to a doctor because she had tearful episodes, or Steph to a doctor because – Lex frowned, and began to search for symptoms.

Outside the pogo stick thumped and ululated like a great ape issuing a territorial warning.

Grace drew a chain and manacles at the foot of the page, and blood dripping in the margin. She said, 'I should hear about what Critchlow is up to with my own ears. And we should see it with our own eyes. Steph could set him up and we could bust in and catch him at it.'

They went out to watch Steph finish.

After several thousand jumps Steph was forced to abandon her attempt at the record. The stick had overheated and scorched the inside thighs of her jeans. The driveway was pockmarked and scattered with loose crumbs of asphalt. Hester consoled Steph – she could always try again tomorrow. Hester could set up the sprinkler in the patch of periwinkle above the drive, and Steph could pogo through the drops every so often, to cool herself down. Then again – Hester thought of a hitch – wet jeans would chafe. She changed the subject. Would they all like pikelets for lunch? Grace too, of course. Pikelets and golden syrup.

Before Grace and Lex took Steph for a walk – with a dollar for Hester's half milk loaf and iceblocks for the girls – Lex stole an envelope, sealed her note, crept, doubled over, up the hill to Critchlow's letterbox, and delivered her dose of poison.

On their way down the hill and around Ivey's Bay, Steph

listened to the older girls discuss what could be done. What effect did they hope a letter would have? Critchlow was hardly likely to write back saying that he'd never do it again. But maybe, next time Steph went up there, he'd send her away.

Neither Grace nor Lex asked Steph why she went up the road – why she didn't just *stop*. Lex took her cue from Grace, to whom this was all new. Grace seemed not to have considered the question.

In games it was decorous to play by the rules – how else could the game be expected to continue? In all games there was an agreement: 'In this world these things are true.' In baseball nobody would steal from third to second, of course; and in Grace's little sister's dolls game no one *commented* that brunette Barbie's husband was a soft toy, a boy Raggedy-Ann (though he wasn't a high-status character, was stuffy and frequently duped). Lex suspected that Grace was acting as though she was playing a game, prolonging the action, playing by the rules, not asking Steph, 'Why not stop going there?'

Lex didn't want to tell Grace that she *had* asked Steph to stop – and Steph hadn't, had sneaked off, later lied about where she was. Steph didn't want to save herself – she wanted to be saved.

And she wanted to talk about it.

It was a hot day so, after they'd bought Hester's milk loaf and it was already sweating oil through its cuff of newsprint, the three girls climbed into the empty concrete milkbox at the front gate of Paremata School. Ever since school milk had been discontinued the box had been unused, and its doors had been removed so that kids couldn't shut themselves in. Grace and Lex sat side by side in the cool, private shade and stretched out their legs, and Steph carefully slotted hers between theirs.

Steph told Grace about Mr Critchlow.

He took the budgie in out of the air and hung its cage above his kitchen sink. He closed his front door. He offered her a hokey-pokey biscuit – softer and soapier than Hester's. He had something to show her, he said. He sat on his narrow, lumpy bed and patted the cover beside him. He unfolded a long concertina of pictures – like *The Silhouette Theatre*, Steph explained – of men and women doing things to each other. It was old, this pamphlet, with the ink gone in its creases; it was silent and insinuating. Critchlow persuaded Steph to take off her panties and did things to her. He licked what he called her pussy until her legs shook, then lay on her in the lumpy bed and tried to put his thing inside her – but he couldn't, he said, she was too dry. Instead he had her put her hand on it.

'That's what happens.'

Lex kept a straight face. She didn't look at Grace. It was important to give no sign that she knew what it meant that Steph's legs would shake – what powerful induction, what inverse volcanic pressure there was, she knew, behind that tremor. Lex pretended not to know. When Steph first told her, bed to bed, in the dark, Lex pretended not to know. And when Steph repeated Critchlow's question, 'Do you ever do this with your sisters?' Lex pretended to be shocked.

Steph had stopped talking. Grace was silent, her chin down on her chest. She looked like a dozing grandmother.

Lex watched her. She would follow Grace's lead: Grace was an outsider, a cooler head.

'When he opens the letter and reads it,' Grace said, 'if he goes red or weak at the knees, he's by himself, nobody sees that.' She thought some more. 'Dad brings home all this lineflow scrap paper from work. Computer paper, with holes at the edge, like film, you know?'

Lex nodded. The only computer she'd seen so far was the one in the huge hot room at the Department of Statistics, on a school trip, three years before. The room had red lights fixed to the ceiling, which, in the event of a fire, would flash for ten seconds before the room flooded with carbon dioxide.

'We can make a big banner out of the computer paper, and hang it on his hedge,' Grace said. 'Make it public.'

Steph said that was a good idea. Then she asked whether they could go back past the shop now, and get their iceblocks.

Grace was puzzled. 'Have I missed something?' Grace asked. Why hadn't Steph defended herself? Didn't Lex tell Grace that Steph had a temper? After all, there was the story about Steph, the Kenny boys, and the octopus.

Lex and Steph were on their way home from school – last year this was, when Lex was a Form Two – when they saw the Kenny brothers bent over some timber object, wet and angular, a disjointed crate perhaps. The brothers had picked up a plank and were scooping with it. They stood side on to whatever it was they were working at, wary and fastidious. As the Keene girls came nearer, Steph suddenly cried out,

'They're trying to kill it!' She left the footpath, slid and tumbled down the bank and onto the shattered concrete boulders of the breakwater. Lex didn't follow but went around by the road to join her sister.

An octopus was clinging to a wet board in the corner of the collapsed crate. Beneath it, where the corner of the crate had dented the sand, was a pool of water, into which the animal was backed, like something in a burrow. The pool wasn't deep, but was dark and oily with octopus ink.

'Leave it alone!' Steph said, then – this had always worked when Hester said it to her – 'How can you be so cruel?'

The boys laughed. They slid the plank under the octopus like a fish-slice under a sticky pikelet, and began to prise it from its anchorage. The animal was terrified and enraged. Lex could see the fear and anger in its alert, remarkably intelligent eyes. She added her voice to Steph's, with less innocent indignation. She could see that an audience, and particularly Steph's distress, added extra spice to the brothers' pleasure.

As the brothers hauled back, the animal's tentacles stretched, and the buried crate creaked. Then the octopus let go and was flung ten feet away on the sand, landing with a wet smack, like a sodden towel thrown down onto a path. Clearly it didn't know where the sea was, because it began to swarm away further inland – and as it did it flushed from apricot to magenta. The boys made after it, and Steph caught at their clothes, crying, her face red with rage. They brushed her off, and stood over the animal, with a board each now, and began, turn and turn about, to beat it on the cringing bag of its head. Steph ran at them again, Lex with her now, but the boys stopped and hefted the planks at them. Lex caught her sister and held her. Steph fought and sobbed, 'I'll kill them. I'm going to kill them.' The Kennys laughed and carried on, but they kept looking back over their shoulders and grinning. They wanted the girls to watch.

'Come on.' Lex began to drag Steph away. 'We're making it worse. We're making it slower.' She managed to remove Steph before the boys began to dismember the animal. She walked her crying and quaking sister away up the hill.

Steph wouldn't have stopped trying to defend the octopus, even if the Kenny brothers beat her. But people are never that brave for themselves, Lex said. If someone picked on her, she always had a sneaking suspicion that she'd provoked it. Like when the three really rough girls in 3Go gave her a hiding because they said her terms-test science score showed them up. 'Tawa's Girls' Dean had me into her office for a word. She wanted to know what I had done to provoke them, what I'd *said*. Which I guess was fair enough. But she wanted an assurance – if she was going to go to the trouble of talking to these girls I had to promise to knuckle down and work really hard next year. I was very humble, very grateful, and I promised. I even thought, for a time, that it was my fault for going about my business in a way that was so different from everyone else's way.'

Grace told Lex not to get overexcited.

'What I mean is, the only time *we* ever fought – you and me – was when I hit your brother because he hit Steph. We were sure of *their* rights. We're never so sure of our

213

own. Steph thinks *she's* the one who started it, see? She went in his house. She thinks she can't let him do what he already has done, then turn around and smack him in the face.'

Grace and Lex regarded Steph walking ahead of them, eating the last of her Popsicle like a corncob, holding it by both ends of its stick. Grace said wasn't it *weird* that all three of them felt that they couldn't do things for themselves. Did everyone feel like that? Was it only natural?

Frank Keene and the Historian were sitting outside in the dusk, side by side on the step of the deck. Lex and Jo came out and sat behind the men, on the door sill, Lex nursing her bottle of stout.

The men were talking about Bill Sutch. How he had felt ousted and shafted – he'd had everything to offer Kirk's Government, and they hadn't wanted any of it.

'Now there are men with torches trampling through his garden in the dark of night.'

The girls got that, though they didn't get 'Economic Brains Trust' or 'Gordon Coates'.

'I'm not really a friend of Bill's. It's my impression he had allies rather than friends,' Frank said.

'A difficult man, and not one you could ever feel you knew. Anyway, I've heard that, when the police gave back the bulk of his papers – mostly papers related to trade deals – the Coates biography was – well – even less complete. But I was told that Bill had shown it to you.'

'Yes. It was quite different from anything else he'd ever written. Experimental. A bit like the New Journalism, with the biographer putting himself in the picture. I don't know

214

why they'd take it – what it had to do with the price of fish.'

The Historian said, 'Hmmm.' He knew more.

'Daddy?' Jo spoke up. 'Who is Gordon Coates?'

'A Prime Minister of New Zealand.'

'He had several illegitimate offspring,' the Historian said. 'Part Maori. The family regards it as a skeleton in their closet. And, you know, they still have a good deal of influence, even in Capital circles.'

Jo inclined towards Lex and whispered, 'Coates of many colours.'

Frank turned right around to look at the Historian, 'Do you think the SIS would do a favour for the Coates family?'

'Possibly. Not the charges, of course – nothing like that – just a sideline in disappearing papers.'

Frank nodded, slowly. Then both men sat quietly sucking on their cigarettes.

Lex put her tongue in the bottleneck and tasted the ferrous brown liquid through its creamy head of foam.

'You wouldn't imagine the Right's memory was as long as the Left's,' Frank said. Then, troubled, 'Do you really think it's likely?'

'I don't know. I'm just going around talking to people. I'll let you know what else I learn.'

'So, these papers were the only copy?' Jo said. Then, to Lex, 'It's scary. It's like *Fahrenheit 451*.' Papers were embryonic books, and the books in Bradbury's book were like people under sentence of death.

'I wonder if it's true,' Frank said again. 'Stories go so quickly from exaggeration to apocrypha.'

Lex asked what apocrypha was and was told she'd find

it on the third shelf of the tall bookcase in the living room. Another version of her father's 'Look it up in the dictionary'. The parental equivalent of 'Buy a streetmap, buddy'.

6

At assembly Lex stopped listening to Stella's Monday morning debrief long enough to look up at the staff on the stage. Miss Sanchez was frowning at her. Lex had forgotten to go to the practice on Saturday morning. She decided not to compound her problem, but to wait for the gym teacher in the Hall foyer. And, having decided, she chose to show her face, but avoid Miss Sanchez's gaze.

'And yesterday I was on the meths,' Stella said, at Lex's ear. 'Me brother and his builder mate, Wayne, gave us rum and a Mogadon. I got all loose, then I spewed, then I went to sleep. I woke up with the *Endeavour* on me cheek, cos I'd been sleeping on money.' Stella was doing her 'I'm a pommy' dialect.

To one side of the stage the school's coat of arms had been defaced. Below Tawa College's motto, 'Do Justly', someone had written, 'You show us Justly, and we'll do him!'

'Loose? Your bowels?' Lex asked.

'Mental.' Stella's voice rose above that of the Deputy Head, who was talking about the latest rubbish drive. If Lex wouldn't pay attention, Stella would get back in character – descend into extravagant rigidity and unresponsiveness, as though to outface the daily dullness. She muttered, '. . . *their blooming flesh for me to hold . . .*' And put her hand in her pocket to draw out her shiny black nylon glove. She put it on, stretched out her arm as she worked her fingers into the glove, formal and deliberate, for all the world like a swordsman in preparation for a duel.

'Sorry,' Lex said.

'Well, since it's you, sunshine,' Stella said, then continued quickly, not just because they'd been asked to rise as the Principal left the stage, but as though she was up on the footplate of a train already moving out of the station. 'I only tried the booze and pills because Dan does it all the time. I wanted to know what the attraction is. And where his *head* is.'

As their row began to file out, Lex followed closely behind Stella. She wanted to know more now, but couldn't think of a question to ask. And she wasn't allowed to take hold of Stella's arm; they only ever touched when Stella cuffed her.

Then Stella said, 'Dan says – knocking it back – that booze raises him above the level of the crowd. And I say, sure, it's like getting a view across the heads of the crowd from the platform of the gallows. I bet our olds can't believe they got such godless kids.' Stella paused and looked at Lex sidelong.

Lex said, 'I'd better wait here for Miss Sanchez. I forgot Saturday's athletics practice.'

'Good for you. Wouldn't want to blow your chance for the lazy prize.'

Someone from Goldman's form class last year had told them how Goldman always staged an alternative prize-giving. There was a 'silliest girl' and a 'stupidest boy'. There were prizes for tardiness, scruffiness and laziness. There was a prize for the class 'swot' and 'goody-good' (and last year the girl who got it cried so long and so hard that her swollen eyelids pressed against the lenses of her glasses).

'I've already written my acceptance speech,' Lex said.

Stella leaned confidingly close, and whispered the whole couplet, '*I love the dead before they're cold, their blooming flesh for me to hold . . .*' and then went on her way.

Lex told Miss Sanchez that her homework had eaten the dog. Then she apologised.

'Keene, you shouldn't be so smart about having no excuse.'

'That wasn't smart, that was *panache* – like the perfume. Panache means flair and style.'

'I know what panache means.'

'What happened was this: my little sister was trying to break the world pogo-stick record. I got involved watching her.'

'Did she?'

'No, the stick overheated and scorched her jeans. Really, she needed *two* sticks and to swap mid-hop – which I

219

bet she could do – like the B52 refuelling mid-air in *Dr Strangelove*.'

The gym teacher just shook her head at this. She asked Lex, 'Do you not want to go to the interschool sports?'

'I do. I'll try to make it to the practices – but there's someone at home I have to take care of.'

Miss Sanchez asked who, and Lex looked at her blankly. Lex said, 'I want to go to the sports and jump. Is there a limit on how many high jumpers Tawa can enter? Am I taking someone's place?'

'No. Kim and Karen have always been streets ahead of all the other girls. But you were *jumping higher than Karen*.'

'I want to just go and jump. I won't get embarrassed. I won't mind what happens. I haven't got a reputation to lose.' Lex managed to sound very happy about it.

There were twelve Third Form classes; 3Go was number eight, the lowest in the language stream. On their second day at college, 3Go, a group of children from as many as ten different primary schools, thrown together in accordance with a recipe, had that recipe explained to them.

It turned out that they had sat a test. The day before, the whole Third Form was welcomed and marshalled through a hall full of stacked stationery to collect what they required, then conducted on a tour of the facilities – art classrooms, wood and metalwork rooms, technical drawing classes, the two canteens and the gym. The tour ended in their rough division, when class-sized groups were settled at desks in the rooms of B Block to 'do some paperwork'.

They had forms to fill in, one with personal information,

health problems, home contacts; another picking optional classes in order of preference. Lex, working her way to the bottom of her pile of forms, found a book of puzzles she supposed was meant to keep her quiet and pass the time. The teacher shushed them to silence. Lex solved four puzzles – turned the page and found shapes instead of words.

Hester knew never to give her middle child a jigsaw puzzle to while away a rainy afternoon. Jigsaws didn't merely bore Lex, they offended her. When she was old enough to explain, she said that she thought it a terrible waste of time to put together a picture that someone else had already seen whole. 'The thing is *done already* and they undo it just so it can be put together again. What's the point?' To Lex all puzzles were the same – things to which someone already had an answer. Word puzzles weren't quite so bad. At least you could amuse yourself with a picture of the man on the train going west at forty-five miles per hour with a basket containing six apples, and imagine what relation he might be to the man going east on a half-hour journey with a pound of butter melting in the hot carriage at the rate of one ounce every six and a half minutes. Whatever the solution was, you could think about the mess of streaky butter on this man's suit, and what his wife might say. An occasional encounter with a puzzle that asked her to sort out an unlike word by some knotty likeness between other words amused Lex. The first four in the booklet were like that – and in making their little logical figures, they required Lex to think about degrees of light, about garments for the extremities, about textures, fruit and vegetables, cooked and raw, cultivated and wild. Then she turned the page and saw a series of hollow and solid geometrical figures.

She upended her pen, and swung it like a divining needle. She lost interest.

Besides, something was happening outside. The day had packed up. The clouds stashed the sun. But before they did, through ten minutes while Lex watched – the pupils of her eyes growing – the light changed in a process like boiling sugar as it caramelised and turned to clear golden toffee. A thunderhead moved along the valley, then opened up as it came near B Block, opened like a big black ledger. Lex was in a classroom on the second floor, and could see the ridge of the roof opposite, also blackish, corrugated asbestos sheets covered in lichen, or possibly tarsealed roofing iron. The roof, dark and wet already from some earlier shower, silvered suddenly in a plane of light that came down, compressed, between volumes of cloud. Gulls flew in to land, one by one, on the spine of the roof. They left the air like boats coming into a harbour ahead of dirty weather. Landed, they made a line of music, uncurled, flexing and rearranging their wings and making their plaintive, two-note rain warning, 'Ray-glib! Ray-glib!'

Lex waited for the thunder. The light was brown now; the toffee burned. A wall of rain swept the gulls from the roof. Lex watched them tumble down the slope, across the guttering, then rise again in the space between the roof and her classroom. She saw their underwings, saw five white crosses diving upward through the torrent; then the rain reached the window of her classroom and everything visible melted.

The teacher turned on another bank of fluorescents. He told them that in five minutes they'd be setting off in this – poor sods.

'My name is Mr Goldman, I'm your form teacher, and you are 3Go. Yesterday you did an IQ test – and according to that test you are all *reasonably* bright, but have trouble concentrating. I hope to be able to address that trouble.'

Lex turned to the girl beside her, who had mottled with anger. 'Did you know that that was an IQ test?'

'Yes. They told us what it was. Weren't you listening?'

'No.'

'I guess you *must* have poor concentration then.'

'I got distracted.'

'Exactly. You have trouble concentrating.'

'I don't think I do. I think I concentrate very hard on the *most interesting* thing going on.'

'But – as me Dad says – if you want to get ahead you've got to buy a hat.'

Lex couldn't fathom that. She stared. A strange girl this – a strange English girl.

Lex jumped for an hour after school. Miss Sanchez and Kim did their best to persuade her to try the Fosbury Flop, but Lex wouldn't jump backwards, wouldn't abandon herself that much. The only time she came close she changed her mind, and twisted herself back mid-jump, like a falling cat getting its forepaws towards the ground. She bruised her chin on the bar. Miss Sanchez gave up on the attempt, and for the last ten minutes let Lex sail over the bar doing her scissors jump.

Kim was piqued – Lex had improved.

Lex said she supposed she'd lost weight.

'You can't afford to.'

'I didn't mean to. And I'm buying a big bag of lollies on the way to the station.'

At Linden Station, Lex found Jo, Ian, and Jo's womanly friend. Jo and the other girl had missed the early train then, counselling Ian, had let the late train go by. The other girl's desire to help Ian wasn't quite as insatiable as Jo's. This girl seemed very pleased to see Lex, and even happier when Lex offered her a lolly. She poked her nose into the bag, breathed on everything, and said, 'Contaminated. All mine!' Then she laughed at Lex's anxious look, took two sweets and gave the bag back.

Ian leapt up. 'Oh God! I have to get home to stand watch over the phone.' He glanced at Lex and said to Jo, 'I hope you haven't told her.'

Jo looked unhappy, but didn't lie.

Ian called her a drongo. He said, 'Haven't you realised that *he* is her friend Stella's brother?' Ian was red, then his blush ebbed as he organised his expression into a masterful sulk. 'You're no help at all,' he told Jo.

'After all the time she puts in listening to you,' Jo's friend said, indignant. 'How *rude*.' This last remark called after Ian as he ran away up the ramp.

Jo defended him. 'Poor Ian. What he's going through is really difficult.'

'Well – he can't expect to get through it without friends. He wants us to approve. We all say we approve, but *I don't approve*. Just because he's gay doesn't mean he has to act like some love pioneer. It's like he wants us to think he's *invented* everything he does. He says he's sharing but he's just showing off.'

The friend helped Jo to her feet. They brushed grit from

their pleated gym skirts. The friend put out her hand for the lolly bag, at the same time saying, 'But you probably shouldn't have told Lex.'

Lex decided not to feel offended. She wasn't being insulted. There was no reason Ian's confidences should include her.

'Loose lips sink ships,' Jo's friend warned. 'All that stuff.'

7

Lex and Grace made their banner on Wednesday night. On Thursday morning, early, Lex went up the road and hung it on Critchlow's hedge, before the school kids began to drain out of their houses and down Bayview and Paremata Roads to the school or station.

On her way home at the end of the day, after another hour of high-jumping practice, Lex rode on one of the underpopulated trains between the two rush hours of three-thirty and five. She had a seat to herself.

She was trying to work out what she felt. It wasn't exactly disappointment, because Miss Sanchez hadn't seemed to have any real expectations of her – but Lex felt she'd been given up on. Lex *couldn't* learn the Fosbury Flop, and Miss Sanchez seemed to have remembered Jo's poor co-ordination. In remembering out loud, the gym teacher had seemed to imply that she thought the Keenes were *bad stock*. 'You're tall for your weight,' Miss Sanchez told Lex. 'That's what's going on. It's a fluke.'

A fluke was circumstantial. Lex wasn't a sport of nature, big-hearted like Phar Lap or Murray Halberg. Miss Sanchez predicted that eventually Lex would 'fill out' and come back down to earth.

What difference did happiness make to the height of her jump? Lex wondered. When she put a little distance between herself and the ground, was still rising, her body closing up on itself – not unlike those cartoon diagrams of cosmic dust spinning into solid bodies, whole planets – then she felt she was *right*, not better, or talented, but whole; she was her own crown, a crown poised *over her own head*. Mid-jump she uncurled, and that was where the competence was, in her preparation for a landing. And the power – the power wasn't in her leap, but in the impact of her intact limbs, an engine of good nature, *happy* as she looked back at the bar, the ruled air, all as still as before. She loved that. She loved it that she *didn't change a thing*, but was suddenly on the other side of it, nothing disturbed.

Lex understood that if she couldn't jump well, then she wouldn't love jumping. If it was a fluke, and it passed, and she couldn't do it any more, then she wouldn't love it any more. She'd wax full, gain weight, fall back before the steepest slope of air. But she'd never forget how it felt, and the feeling was a scale, like the centimetres marked off on the uprights of the jump, against which she could measure any future flukes – how *whole* her competence, how *high* her joy.

After Miss Sanchez mentioned Jo's problems, she began to talk about remedial Phys Ed. When Jo was in the lower forms, and still in her power, Miss Sanchez had mentioned remedial Phys Ed to Jo's father at a parent-teacher evening. Lex listened and tried not to take it personally. She didn't suppose she'd be asked to sign on. Remedial Phys Ed didn't sound nearly as pleasant as the remedial reading programme she had been cast out of – like Eve from Eden – earlier that year.

At Paremata School Lex had been promoted to the highest spelling group by virtue of her written comprehension. When she got to college, equipped only with her stunned and wandering cursive, and her patchy spelling, Lex was regarded by her English teacher as rather backward. Anyone who wrote so badly must need remedial reading.

Lex arrived in Mr Coffin's study on a wet day in early winter, with her English folder and her copy of *Shane*. There were six other Third Formers sitting in a circle around a one-bar electric heater. One was a classmate, a sweet boy who fidgeted all the time (and who, at the end of the year, was the recipient of Goldman's 'stupidest boy' award). The rest were strangers.

For the first lesson Lex simply listened. She thought the other kids were only pretending not to understand the stories they were asked about. By the lesson's end, however, she decided that, if that was what was done here, what was required, then there had been a mistake – *she* didn't need any help. Lex liked Mr Coffin; she liked his white hair and big-knuckled red hands, his patient, succinct questions, the pains he took not to explain everything, but to help the kids to explanations. He reminded her of *The Young Lawyers* on TV. Like Mr Coffin, a lawyer questioning a witness might ask, 'What kind of man is Shane?' and, 'Why do you think he sits with his back to the wall?'

In the next lesson Lex was expected to talk. They read a short story by Ray Bradbury. Mr Coffin asked questions, interesting questions and, since she was allowed, Lex answered. When Mr Coffin said, 'Are we supposed to think the boyfriend is dangerous?' Lex, cheerful and engaged, said, 'I think we're meant to think *two* things – the girl is being twitchy *and* she might be right to be scared of him. He's worked on his body so hard that he's left no room for his soul. The hand springs he's squeezing at the end make him sound like a machine.'

Mr Coffin looked at Lex in a way that wasn't encouraging. She decided she hadn't proven her point, took a deep breath to charge her brain and went on. 'It's like that story "The Tell-Tale Heart", it might be the murderer's conscience making him hear things, or it could be a haunting. This is another either-way-you-look-at-it story. Maybe Ray Bradbury watched body-builders and thought, if they cared so much about lifting weights, what room did they have to care about other stuff? There's a bit about Ray Bradbury's life in one of my Dad's *Best of SF* collections. It says he lived in Venice. Not the Venice in Italy, the Venice in California. There are muscle men on Venice Beach; I saw some photos in my Aunt Paulie's *Photography Today*.' Lex was trying to explain that, if you could prove that someone – a writer – saw a certain thing, then perhaps it was possible to guess what they thought about it.

The other kids looked gloomy. Mr Coffin asked Lex to

read a paragraph out loud. She liked the last one, so read that.

Mr Coffin asked her to stay after class. He saw the other pupils off, then sat back down. Lex told him she liked his office, it was more of a sitting room. 'That's what my mother said to my Aunt about her cottage on Mount Vic. "You can't call this a living room, Paulie, this is a parlour."' Lex blushed – because they'd been talking about books she'd forgotten herself, and her family had spilled over into everything. 'Your room is the warmest in the school, I think. Everywhere else I have to lean on the radiators.'

Mr Coffin pointed at the radiator, which was working – Lex could see the waving seaweed transparencies its heat made against the shelved books. 'My heater is supplementary.' He blinked at her. He appeared to be waiting for a sign. Then he added, 'Old bones. I'm five years past retirement. I keep this up because I enjoy it.'

He enjoyed teaching; he was good at it. Lex smiled at him and swung her legs.

'You shouldn't have been sent to me. You're an able and sophisticated reader. You must realise there's been a mistake. Why do you think your teacher made this mistake?'

'My spelling is rotten. I'm careless, I'm told.'

'Are you?'

Lex shrugged.

Mr Coffin imitated her shrug and said, 'She's careless – but what does she care.'

Lex laughed. She said, 'I'm not *neat*. Girls are always neat. My teacher can't read my handwriting.'

'You are going to have to learn to write legibly.'

Lex made some expression of concession. Then she

asked, 'Can't I come back?'

'No. It's too discouraging for the others. Those boys really need my help.'

'Why are they all boys?'

Mr Coffin said, 'That's a good question.' He didn't attempt to answer it, though, or ask her to speculate. She felt she was being expelled from the best game she'd played in weeks.

Mr Coffin stood by the door to see Lex out. She gave a last sidelong look at the bookshelves, the swivel chair with timber arms, the orange element of the heater, the warmth of which made her slit her eyes. 'It's nice here,' she said, then went out.

When Lex reached her gate she saw that there were several small scraps of paper shining in the darkness of Critchlow's hedge, the corners of pages, twigs through the perforations.

Jo followed Lex around as Lex cleared the table and stacked dishes. Jo was speculating in a graphic way about what Ian might be up to this very minute.

Hester was still at the table with her after-dinner cigarette, her hand on her bread and butter plate, at which Lex had made an absentminded pass. Hester told Jo, 'Go bag your head. You're being terribly porky.'

'What do you mean?' Jo said, her nose already lighting up – the over-sensitive skin where she'd had impetigo in childhood.

'Vulgar.'

'You only say that because you're a prude!' Jo yelled, then burst into tears and ran out of the room.

Hester sighed, raised both eyebrows at Lex and shrugged first one then the other shoulder.

'I think you weren't meant to be listening.' Lex grabbed Hester's plate – too fast, and a half-inch cylinder of ash, the mummy of a cigarette, rolled onto the table, came to a standstill and disintegrated.

'Then she should moderate her voice.'

'Jo thinks people are prudish if they don't want to talk to her about sex. She seems to forget that when you and Dad are with your old tramping club friends you make filthy jokes.'

'She hasn't hurt my feelings, Lex. But I do feel a little awkward hearing things about Ian which his own mother doesn't know.' Hester told Lex that she'd give Jo five minutes, then go and tell her to wash her face and come and dry the dishes for Lex. Lex said she'd ask Steph to help her. She wanted to take a good look at her little sister. Steph had been rather distant and casual at dinner.

'No. Nonsense. Jo isn't going to get out of the dishes just because she's weepy.'

Jo came out of her room and stopped her sister as Lex left the bathroom with a hot-water bottle clutched to her ribs.

'That phone call was Ian,' Jo said. The phone had rung fifteen minutes before.

Jo leaned against the doorframe and shivered. 'He was crying. He wasn't very coherent. He wanted me to meet him. He couldn't talk properly – his asthma – but he did remember that our phone is bugged.' Jo's tone was faintly self-important, which Lex suspected meant Jo was having trouble believing this was really happening, and she was actually involved. 'He said he'd meet me on Paremata Station, that *he'd* come to see *me*, and you know what a sponge he is.'

Lex nodded.

'It's the Catholic boyfriend – he rung up drunk and crazy and threatened to kill himself. That's all I got out of Ian.' Jo glanced along the hall towards their parents' room, where Frank was in bed already. 'We were discussing criminal matters and I started to worry about the phone.'

'Are you going to sneak out?' Lex was impressed.

'No. I can't – I told him I can't. I'm not going to rush down to the station and hang about, having to hide from hoons and creeps, on the promise of Ian turning up. He probably wouldn't. He'd probably calm down and go to bed and forget to tell me he didn't need me. He does things like that. Besides, I don't want him crying on my shoulder half the night. I've got school tomorrow; so has he. I told him I couldn't. Do you think I should have?'

'Not if it scares you.'

'If you had been there when I took the call I could have asked you to go with me.'

Lex was glad she wasn't there and hadn't been asked. She was surprised that Jo hadn't agreed to meet Ian. It had been her impression that Jo was devoted to Ian. And the Jo who had led the expeditions of Lex's childhood wouldn't have hesitated to run out in the dark after knowledge or adventure. When had this timidity appeared – amid the noise, complaints, and tears of adolescence – this tepid inertia?

Lex balanced, her bare feet crossed and warming each other. She frowned at her sister.

'Do you think I should have?' Jo said.

Lex shook her head.

'He's having a drama,' Jo said. 'I take him very seriously and he never – you know – returns the compliment.'

From the kitchen Hester called out, 'Jo! Let your sister go to bed!'

When the lights were out in their bedroom, Steph told Lex that she'd been 'up the road'. She'd wanted to see what Critchlow thought of the banner on his hedge. Critchlow told Steph no one had seen it. He'd come out into his front yard early that morning. 'He sometimes watches the kids go to school. And he's always out there at three-thirty – have you noticed, Lex?'

Lex had noticed that Critchlow swept the concrete, or weeded the windowbox, or polished his brass doorstep, or just stood, lips pursed, flicking the bars of the budgie's cage, while the kids climbed the road past his gate.

Critchlow had heard the banner unpick at one end and begin to flap in the breeze. He tore it down.

'He told me to tell you that it's against the law. That "threatening letters" are a form of blackmail.'

Lex felt lightheaded – even lying down. This was all so strange, so puzzling.

'He said, "I'm not afraid of your sister and her friend."'

Critchlow asked Steph then, what did she think her mother would say if she found out about the letter? If she found out that it was Steph who came to visit him – sometimes twice a day? Then he told Steph she was a naughty girl. 'I'm naughty because I've let you think he makes me,' Steph said. 'And I haven't told you that he gives me lifts to school. That's why he found the banner. He came out to get me. He said I should tell you that.'

Steph had changed her story.

There is a word, Lex thought, *there is a way to think about this.*

'Lex?'

She was falling into herself, over and over, as though she were a concertina of paper lace, little figures with linked hands, back to back, face to face.

'Lex?'

'Why do you go up there?' Lex asked.

Steph said she didn't know. It was just something she was doing. 'Like jumping on my pogo stick. I don't have anyone to play with. You're always out on the water with Grace. Again, like last summer. You won't play with me except to make me hold the end of the stick when you jump. That's boring.'

When Lex had been in Standard Four, in her first year at Paremata School, and Steph was still a primer, Steph had spent four weeks home sick with bronchitis. When Steph came back to school she was out of step with her classmates, and she was lonely. She would stand, looking limp, at the edges of games, waiting to be included. Or she would perch on the bottom wire of the fence between the playground and Paremata Crescent, and cry to go home, cry for her mother. After a few days of this, Lex left her set of friends, their perpetual game of four-square, and began to play with Steph, at interval and lunchtime. Lex's friends came to her – a delegation – and they took her aside, walked her to the end of the field, and said what they had to say.

Consensual home truths. They weren't prepared to play with anyone who spent all their time with a primer. 'You have to choose,' they said. Lex told them, in lofty tones, that there was no choice. 'This is my sister. And do you think I want to play with a pack of selfish girls who expect me to choose?' Well, if she was going to be like that, they said . . .

Frank said this policy was 'ostracism', and that nations did it to each other. 'It's often very effective. But you must stick to your guns.'

Lex stopped speaking to her friends. She played with Steph. Resentfully. She invented a stalking game. Steph was supposed to creep up on her, track her around school buildings – but Lex kept so far ahead of her sister that she was always behind her. For whole half-hours she watched Steph search for her, solitary among flights of kids about this or that game, anxious, trudging around buildings, turning and searching.

After a week of this, Lex's friends came back to her – a delegation again – to apologise. They were wrong. Of course they understood that she had to look after her little sister. But why didn't they all go and talk to some of the girls in Steph's class? Get them to adopt her? Three of them went to prevail upon Felice Brent. Lex said to Felice, 'Before Rachel came to live with you, you and Steph were buddies. I know you're a kind girl, Felice, couldn't you include Steph in your games again? And if she doesn't seem interested, if she's slow or grumpy, it's only because she's been so ill.'

'Very ill,' added one of Lex's friends.

It worked. Felice took Steph in hand. And Lex, waiting at the edge of the four-square for her turn, for someone to fumble the ball, could look down the crowded corridor of netball courts laid end to end, at Steph swaying back and forth, with her hands up, about to brave a churning jump-rope.

Lex felt herself still falling, not one prolonged fall, but fall after fall, as though she were on a rope, a chain on a mountain face, a chain of Lexes, falling successively, each pulling another off the mountain, with someone below shouting at her: 'Hold! Hold that man!'

Lex made a decision without having any ideas – that was faith, and faith stopped her fall. She would think of something to do with Steph – something better than stand-ing holding up one end of the high jump – games and expeditions like those games and expeditions Jo had pursued or invented, including her. Games of ghosts, dinosaurs, millionaires, madmen and angels, expeditions up the line to Avalon, or down the line to Rosebud, the adventures and the stories that were air and food to Lex.

Steph said her name again. Lex's sister was sitting up in bed, in tears. Lex had no notion of how long she'd been silent.

Lex said, 'I can't make him stop. I can't make him send you away. We have to tell Mum.'

Steph wept.

'Mum will stop him,' Lex promised. And she thought, 'She'll stop you.'

'Steph,' she said, 'I can't do anything about this. You tell me things, but you sneak off. You won't lie to Mum. Once you've told her – that will be that.'

'No, I can't.'

237

'I'm not going to do anything more for you, Steph. Either you tell, or I'll tell.'

Steph said all right, she'd tell, but Lex had to go with her. 'And just Mum, not Dad.'

'Yes. Tomorrow, after school, before Dad comes home.'

And Lex thought, later their mother would tell their father, and together *they* could make something of it.

A big fuss. Sense.

8

A friend of Lex's and Stella's, a girl from the science bench, was leaning on Lex's locker, waiting for her. It was five minutes until the form meeting. The girl shuffled to one side, moved like a hinge to hem Lex in so that when the locker was open the girl spoke into it.

Stella wasn't at school today, the girl said. She'd stopped by Stella's house as she sometimes did so that they could walk together, and Stella's Dad answered the door. 'Stella's brother has died. And I just saw Goldman talking to the Head. They both looked very grim, so I guess Goldman will say something about it to the form.'

The girl stepped back as Lex closed her locker. She trailed Lex along the corridor and upstairs to their class.

'They might let us off for the funeral. He was a Tawa College old boy.'

Lex wondered how this would affect Stella's enjoyment of Alice Cooper. She was surprised to find herself incapable of sympathy. Perhaps she'd left it – something visible – lying on her pillow, like that sick woman in a film she'd seen whose cancer treatment caused her to wake up one morning in a nest of her own cast-off hair.

Goldman had no more information – or none he was prepared to share with the whole class. When he'd dismissed them, and the majority had sloped off for first period, and as their desks filled with Goldman's Fifth Form history class – a sober bunch, three weeks away from their exam – a small group of Goldman's girls went up to question him further.

Stella's brother had been hit by a truck while out walking at night. 'He fell in front of it,' Goldman said.

'Was he drunk?' one girl asked.

'I have no idea.'

'If we wanted to go to the funeral we could, eh?'

'I imagine so. There will be a notice at assembly tomorrow.'

Lex, who was at the back of the group, saw Goldman's irritation at the way they exchanged looks. Perhaps he saw opportunism. She knew they were reaching an agreement on whether they were satisfied with what he had told them.

'OK, Sir,' said one girl, in a way that might mean either 'thanks' or 'we'll let you off for now'.

They didn't go to class. It turned out that one of them had been sweet on Dan. She got weepy. And so they skipped class and went, as a group, to the girls' toilets in D Block.

A moment after they arrived, the three Fourth Formers in the far cubicle climbed down off the toilet seat and pulled their hands – holding cigarettes – back through the louvres. The girls from 3Go sat down, lining the wall under the polished steel mirror. Someone gave the weepy one a cigarette, but didn't light up herself.

Lex looked down at her legs in the line of legs, her Charlie Browns and theirs, the row of dirty crepe soles and frayed shoelaces. She was grateful for the likeness, and the warmth of bodies either side of her own.

One of the Fourths came out to say that the hall monitor had already been through; they'd paid her off. 'You turds gave us a real turn. What's wrong with *her*?'

'Her boyfriend's dead.'

'No shit?' The Fourths were impressed. They stood and talked a while, put in their hair elastics and went out to class.

The Third Formers shared their troubles to soothe each other. One was still missing her Nana who died in July. Another's brother had been in a car crash, had whacked his head on the cigarette lighter and had, ever since, a creepy dent on his forehead and a vicious temper. Lex told her classmates that her little sister was being molested by the old man up the road and they were going to tell their mother. Two Linden girls exchanged stories about the flasher who waited along the road. 'He lies in the long grass and groans. First time I saw him I thought he was hurt so I went over to see and he moaned: "I've got a Big One coming on!"'

'Revolting!'

Laughter.

At the end of the row nearest the door the prettiest girl in 3Go said that her boyfriend and his friend had raped her.

'It was in his parents' house when they were out. We were on the couch watching TV and I noticed Max and Andy whispering. Then they just jumped on me.'

They all looked at her. The whole row turned her way with their mouths open like the laughing clowns at Luna Park.

'I couldn't do anything.'

'But I saw you at the pictures with Max on Friday night.'

'Yes. Then we broke up on Saturday.'

'That's when it happened?'

'No – it happened the Saturday before last. We made up. But I didn't really want to. So.'

'Jesus!' someone said.

'He apologised,' the girl said. 'I didn't know what to do.'

Lex looked at her feet and had a kind of hallucination, a hallucination that included her feet. The world rolled out like a red carpet before her, blazing like a long cut filling with blood. And the world said: *This is how I am.* The world chanted, in brutal exultation, as soft and deafening as the very nearest sound: *Behold me! Behold thou me!*

Lex closed her eyes and, eyes closed, reached down and pulled her socks up to her knees, then sat back and drew her cuffs down over her knuckles.

When Lex got home she found Steph waiting for her on the steps. Her sister sat, legs dangling, her forehead pressed to the steel handrail. The peg bucket was at Steph's side and she had been making herself a thorny chaplet of linked spring-clip pegs.

Steph said she had spoken to their mother.

Lex asked Steph had their mother heard her out? Had Steph told her what Critchlow had done, how, how often, and how Lex had handled it?

Steph stared at her sister, stony, but like a stone on which the sun was coming up. She coloured gradually as though blood was being crushed up into her head. She said, 'Mum wants to speak to you. I told her that I didn't want him to go to prison.'

Lex went inside. Hester was in the kitchen, cutting up gravy beef for the cats, who were milling around her legs, as humpbacked and happy as dolphins.

Hester said that she had told Steph that she must simply *not go up there again*. Steph had seemed very distressed that the old man would be sent to prison, and that if he did go to prison he'd die there. Hester had spent a long time reassuring her about that. Steph must avoid Crit. If she stayed away from him there wouldn't be another incident. Hester couldn't believe that none of her neighbours had warned her that the old man was still fiddling with girls – they never said a thing, and here she was with *three* daughters. 'As for you,' Hester said to Lex, 'you should know better.' Lex's poison-pen letters were childish and half-baked. And criminal – didn't Lex understand that there were laws against that kind of thing? And Lex should not have involved Grace Hutton – the two of them egging each other on.

'From now on please try to be more sensible. Both of you. And Lex, I don't expect to hear anything more of this sort of nonsense. No more threats. You steer clear of him too.'

Lex was dismissed. Her mother was disappointed in her.

She retreated to her room and stood watching the mice, who were running about busily on top of the dresser, their tails high. Hester didn't think the mice should be cooped up all day.

After a minute Steph joined her, sat on her bed, pulled off her shoes and applied herself to rethreading a broken shoelace so that its ends would still be long enough to make a knot. She said, 'Did Mum say she'd have a word with Dad?'

Lex couldn't remember. Her memory of the day seemed to be crumbling, like a cake whose cook has forgotten to add eggs to the mix. Perhaps Hester *had* said she'd speak to Frank. Lex said to her sister, 'I'm sure she'll tell him. And I hope you listened to her, Steph. You *must* stop going up there.'

Lex lay down, rolled over and faced the wall and, sellotaped to it, a page out of *Pink*: Bowie in the electric blue jumpsuit with the black fake-fur collar, his mismatched eyes and pale powdered chest. There was a face that knew a thing or two.

Lex supposed her mother was right to tell her off – must be right since Lex found that she didn't feel indignant about being told off. And, when she thought about the flaming skulls and daggers dripping blood, she *did* feel ashamed of her poison pen.

If she felt anything.

In a minute she would go and talk to Jo. She put her hands between her knees and pressed them flat. Lex supposed she felt relief, but that Steph's telling their mother had turned out to be a kind of anticlimax. Lex had been afraid that her mother would question her – but Hester seemed to get the gist of the letter she and Grace had written, and didn't need anything spelled out.

Lex hoped Steph hadn't made her accusation as though making a confession. If she had, that would account for Hester's briskness. In Lex's opinion, Hester's 'no nonsense' wasn't the right approach. Steph's repeated visits to Critchlow weren't *nonsense*, even if they didn't make sense.

'In a minute,' Lex thought, her mind thickening and darkening like a caramel on a slow simmer. In a minute she'd go speak to Jo.

Jo's voice: 'They're both asleep.'

Hester's voice, further off: 'Well, tell them that dinner will be on the table in five minutes. Could one of them please set it? Whoever's turn it is.'

Steph rolled off her bed and slouched out of the bedroom.

'Jo?'

Jo sat down behind Lex's crooked knees.

Lex told her older sister about Steph and Critchlow, and about Hester's reaction to Steph's confession. Lex was considering how to explain her worries about Steph's reticence. She was thinking about how Steph's story had come to *her* piecemeal, and hoping Steph had told Hester *all* of it – when Jo said something, her tone very certain and assertive. But Lex was head-first down some muffling hole and couldn't hear properly. For a minute, she only felt the vibrations of her sister's voice through her spine.

'The problem with our society,' Jo was saying, 'is its hypocrisy. People should be more frank and open.' Lex's sister was speaking as if about the general public, saying how people should *generally* behave – as if Hester's reaction was somehow typical, not of Hester, but of people, or society in general.

Lex sat up and backed against the wall, her legs drawn up under her chin. She tried to catch Jo's eye, said, 'Listen,' several times and then spoke into the pause the word made – subsequent words broadening the pause into a silence. She said that she knew why Steph kept going back to Critchlow. She knew and hadn't been able to explain to Hester what she knew, because of *how* she came to know it. She hadn't been able to talk about it, to ask Hester what Steph had told her, to say that there was something *more*, something vital that Hester should understand.

'Steph told me that Critchlow said, "Do you ever do this with your sisters?" I kept my mouth shut. Jo, do you remember how he caught us in his orchard that time?'

Critchlow had appeared above them on the slope. He came from a door in the mildewed back wall of his house, and moved quickly between the trees. He didn't yell, just asked, 'What are you doing?' But he was an adult, so the girls heard adult shock and indignation in his voice. Lex was over the fence before Jo got up off her back and retrieved her panties out of her gumboot tops, pulled them up and ran.

Jo winced. 'So, because Critchlow saw us playing *rudies*, he figured our little sister wants to play with him?'

'Yes.' But this wasn't what Lex was trying to communicate. It was all about knowledge – forbidden fruit, like the 'knowledge' of Original Sin – what Critchlow saw and supposed he knew, what Lex had been taught by Jo and couldn't let on she knew – facts and moments culminating in *something* that happened, something unrepeatable and as purely circumstantial as the best height Lex could leap. It had nothing to do with the hypocrisy of society. It was all circumstances and secrets.

Lex heard her mother's footfall outside the door. She saw a shape – her mother – look around the door. Blurred. The whole room was out of focus, as though Lex's gaze had fallen short, or fixed itself on an imaginary screen of air that divided the room between the beds and the door, between her mother's face and her own.

Hester said that their dinners were on the table and getting cold.

9

Lex tried to find her father with her eyes. There he was, like a sleeping bird, head tucked down into the wing of his jacket. He got the cigarette lit, his mouth let off one syllable of a smoke signal, then he buttoned his jacket and wedged his hands into his armpits. The ground was dry but the wind cold. Lex sat low to the ground with her bare legs folded up into her jersey, stretching it. The wind funnelled in through two hills, Newtown and Berhampore, inner-city suburbs set so close together that Lex couldn't see any need for distinction. She didn't often get into the city, and never out this way, since the Zoo lost the charm it had kept throughout her childhood. These steep streets and crammed-together white weatherboard houses were unsettling and strange to her, so that she found herself keeping her father in sight at all times. Her father, his car keys, the car, the jeans on the back seat that she'd had on over her gym shorts – modesty, bodily safety, her ride, her way home.

Kim came over and reminded Lex that there was a distinction between keeping warm and warming up. She invited Lex to do a few warm-up stretches, then tapped Lex's ankle with the toe of her own shoe in order to winkle Lex out of the shell of her jersey. Lex got up, watched Kim, followed suit, rolled her shoulders, shook her legs.

'You have to stay warm or you'll be eliminated.'

There were now only eight girls jumping. Miss Sanchez had already been taken to task about Lex's scissors jump. Three years earlier that was all the trainers had – a scissors jump and no tricks in their books. The Fosbury Flop was something they all had to prove, locally, and they were only just beginning, at this level of competition, to get the height they'd hoped for. Now here was Shelley Sanchez of Tawa College with a tiny, gravity-defying *throwback*.

'I'm enjoying this,' Kim said. She already had her first in the hurdles, and was in a good mood. She squatted beside Lex and gave Lex's calf muscles a brisk rub. 'I think I'd prefer you to beat me if it means beating that Jensen girl from Wellington East.' Kim stood and put her hand in her pocket, drew out two sugar lumps and offered them to Lex on her flat palm as though Lex were a horse. She asked about Goldman's prize-giving. 'It's famous, you know, very democratic – and there's real distinction in some of the prizes.'

Lex said if that was democracy it was a *see you on the*

dark side of the moon kind of democracy. 'Goldman was even-handed. We were all useless, even the good students. Well, no, that's not quite right – the kids with no real distinguishing features, good or bad, they didn't get prizes. I got the "laziest" prize. I made a speech about how I hadn't done anything to deserve it, and how my wasted potential and lack of effort just couldn't come up to that of a friend, and I gave it to her. Pretty limp, really. Mathis put on a headband with a black wool plait and seagull feather stuck to it, and imitated that Cheyenne girl who turned down Marlon Brando's Oscar. And the girl who got "swot" cried all day.'

Kim told Lex she should run on the spot; she was covered in goose bumps. Then the older girl went off to take her own turn.

Lex pumped her legs and arms, then followed Kim to the jump. She made it. No one clapped or sighed. The Sports were short on audience. Although the whole field was alive with activity – sprints, relays, long and high jumps – competitors, coaches and judges were the only people nearby, and the stand was largely empty.

Miss Sanchez came up to her jumpers, laid an arm across Kim's shoulders and said, 'You've both made the final four. You get two jumps at five-eight. Tie your hair back again, please, Kim. If you do your best, girls, I think you can both do better than Jensen.'

Lex stood shivering until it was again her turn. She looked for her father, but couldn't see him. The day had darkened and she was having trouble with distances – judging them – as she discovered when she jumped and felt the bar behind her as a blur in the air. She heard the few onlookers moan, either thrilled or thwarted, and looked back. The bar trembled, but stayed put.

Kim said, 'That's it for Tawa then. We've both reached our ceiling.'

They watched the Jensen girl make another muscular flourish above the bar.

Again Lex looked around for her father, and this time he waved to her; he'd moved down the stand, into a more sheltered spot. Perhaps he'd been back to the car, because he was wearing his beret. Kim followed Lex's gaze and said her Dad looked very continental – was he an artist? After all, Lex's sister Jo hung out with all those artistic kids – half of whom were in black armbands at Dan Morrissey's funeral the other day. But Dan was only a builder's mate, so what was the story there? Those same kids had been at the Church production of *Godspell* last month, all in toppers and frockcoats and white stage make-up, and in the interval the stage manager had dashed out to ask everyone to pray because – and Kim quoted – 'The forces of evil are among us!' Would you believe.

Jo had told Lex that, at the funeral, she and the other Sixths had packed tightly around Ian, to hold him up, and suppress his trembling so that it would be less perceptible. Ian wasn't even going to go, Jo said, but the whole local dramatic society attended, so he was obliged to. Obliged to listen to all the Christian mystified-in-the-face-of-awful-accidents carry-on.

'The forces of evil,' Kim repeated to herself, snorted. 'So, how is your friend Stella coping?'

'Her Dad rung me yesterday and asked me to ask her out. We went to *The Big Boss*. She's swapping allegiances from Alice Cooper to Bruce Lee.'

'I asked how she is, not what she's into.'

'She's sad. She hasn't a clue why it happened.'

'All right. There's no need to be touchy.'

They stood in silence until it was again Kim's turn. Kim clipped the bar with her shoulder and took it down with her. There was a groan of sympathy, then a smattering of clapping.

Miss Sanchez led Lex to her place in the runway, her hand on Lex's shoulder. Lex said, 'I've jumped this height at home – higher – well over my own head. I'm not scared of the bamboo, but this bar hurts.'

'Then clear it.'

When Miss Sanchez left her side Lex crouched, unlaced her sneakers and pulled them off. She stripped her socks off too. The ground was warm through the balding grass. She saw the adjudicator give her the nod. Miss Sanchez called out her name, but Lex was running already. She swung in, slowed down, came down hard on her right foot and took off, left leg first. Her whole body folded like a fan slapped expressively in a gloved palm – after the gesture a pause – she had everyone's attention. Then the wind came to the party, picked her up and blew her over the hard bar and dropped her onto the squabs. She lay still. Miss Sanchez and the adjudicator both came and stood above her.

The adjudicator said, 'Didn't you hear me? I meant your *feet*.' She pointed again with her nose – the nod – her hands seemed to be welded to her clipboard. 'The jump isn't official with bare feet.'

Why, Lex asked. Was it easier barefoot?

'The Fosbury Flop *is*, possibly, for athletes with poor technique.' The adjudicator sounded apologetic. 'Anyway, rules are rules. Can you not do it again with your shoes on?'

'No.'

'Come on, Keene, try it and see,' Miss Sanchez coaxed.

'Can't you just say that the Jensen girl has won? I'll take second. I don't want to knock the bar down.'

'You won't be taking second, Lex. Your last official jump puts you behind Kim. In third. Come on, Lex, jump again.' Miss Sanchez plucked at the shoulder of Lex's shirt.

'I don't want to knock the bar down,' Lex said. Then she began to cry.

'There's nothing to cry about,' the adjudicator said. She sounded distressed. Then she spoke sternly to Miss Sanchez. 'This girl is clearly unwilling to compete further.'

'You'll have to take a third, Lex.' Miss Sanchez seemed to threaten.

Lex nodded. She wiped her eyes, pushed and pushed the tears into the hair at her temples. She couldn't understand why she was crying. She didn't *feel* anything.

Miss Sanchez helped her up. Lex decided it was advisable to limp. She didn't want to have to explain her tears. Then there was a fuss in which she had to decide which foot to favour, and where to guide them to apply the ice. The Jensen girl came over and shook her hand. Kim told her what an idiot she was to remove her shoes. Someone produced a yellow ribbon printed in green: Wellington Regional Secondary School Athletics. Miss Sanchez pinned the ribbon on her shirt. Kim showed Lex *her* blue ribbon and ten-dollar book token.

Frank appeared and offered his daughter an arm. He asked Miss Sanchez, was it only a minor sprain? There was no visible bruise or swelling.

Lex could see her father thinking, 'This woman is an American.' He'd been unprepared for an American, for the gym teacher's sleek completeness. He looked irritated. Frank knew a thing or two about 'sprains', had carried injured people off the great white causeway of the Tasman Glacier. In defiance either of the gym teacher's minimising, or possibly of his own bad back, Frank picked his daughter up and carried her from the field and into the carpark. As he walked he complained how 'that woman', in her competitive spirit, was losing sight of safety.

Frank put Lex down by the car and opened the door for her. 'Anyway. Well done, Lex. But why *did* you take off your shoes?'

'I wanted to lose ballast.'

He said, 'Is that right?' Then he reminded her, 'Seatbelt, Curly.'

Lex had thought that, on the ride home, when they were alone, and once the stresses of her performance were over, her father might ask her about Mr Critchlow.

But, apparently, Hester hadn't told him.

Grace and Lex stood side by side on the shore, their arms folded. Grace remarked that the sky looked like cold porridge, and the Bay wasn't very tempting.

Lex said that she had only been able to come out because Steph had one of her friends over. The kids were entertaining themselves by going around the house killing flies by firing rubber bands at them. Lex had promised to be back in time to make a tally. 'We won't be able to go out on the water by ourselves so often, Grace. When the water is warmer we can dub Steph. She could straddle the stern.'

Grace accepted this without question or any sign of surprise. She just stood, hugging herself and smiling at Lex. Maybe smiling – but the expression was warmer than a smile, and had more in it than amusement or friendliness.

'Anyway,' Lex said, 'are we allowed to go out yet?'

'Are we being watched now? I doubt it. When Barnes called to report that we'd nearly capsized Dad was more embarrassed than worried. If my parents were really concerned they'd buy life-jackets.'

'You sound like Jo, she thinks most adults are only motivated by embarrassment.'

Grace said, 'Uh huh.' After a moment she added, 'You must be angry with your mother.'

Lex shook her head. She tried to think of something to say, and when she did think of something, and said it, her voice sounded thin and pinched, like a stereo with the sound out in one channel. 'We shouldn't expect too much of anyone,' she said.

Grace said, 'Don't say that. Don't *you* say that.'

Jo was shut in her room writing poetry – 'my life is an island of confusion in a sea of nothing' – so only Lex went out to eavesdrop on her father and the Historian. As she passed her mother Hester said, 'It's rather chilly out there now, but perhaps they're pretending the house is bugged. Ask them if they want another beer, pet.'

Lex asked, then fetched another bottle and the opener. Frank topped up the glasses. He asked Lex had she had her stout? She had. He sent her in to get another glass and poured her some lager, explaining to the Historian that his gravity-defying daughter had come third in the girls' high jump at the regional school sports. They raised their glasses to her.

The Historian put his glass down and rubbed his temples. Back to business. He said, 'I've never felt I knew Bill. I'd like to be able to say I can't put any credit in the story.'

'You're saying you think Bill *was* passing secrets?'

'Well – it's difficult. We have to get past this notion that he has to be – politically – as pure as the driven snow in order for us to be able to say that he's been treated shabbily. Frank, the rumour is that what Bill passed on to the Russians was a dossier he'd compiled – as a kind of hobby really – a dossier of compromising facts about various politicians and senior civil servants. It has always been one of Bill's oddities – perhaps part of his misanthropy – this love of salacious gossip. I've heard it said that he wasn't above tailing cabinet ministers into public toilets to see what they got up to.'

Lex said, flatly, 'Oh. More creepy sex secrets.'

The Historian frowned at her.

'Do you believe the rumours?' Frank asked him.

'No. But it worries me that I find I have to give the rumours no credit in order to be on Bill's side. He shouldn't have to be completely innocent. That's a moral crudity. It's like – now that we're all supposed to appreciate Baxter he's been rehabilitated. The sainted Hemi. His poor personal hygiene is now Saint Francis of Assisi territory.'

Lex said, 'Dad and another Tramping Club friend said that when Baxter holed up in someone's flat after a party he used the wastepaper basket as a toilet so that he wouldn't have to leave the room.' She blushed as she reported this.

'Student party,' Frank explained. 'He had a woman with him. Didn't want to go to the lav in case she gave him the slip. Took a crap in the wastepaper basket. The later fleas-in-the-saintly-beard stuff is his own myth-making. But, anyway, can it matter how a man smelled once he's in the ground?' Frank gave his daughter a stern look.

'But you follow my meaning, don't you?' the Historian said. 'In this country if you stick your head out you'd better make sure you're wearing a halo.'

'Mate, a halo is just a treble on the dartboard.'

Lex interrupted again. Did her father remember how he used to argue with Baxter about original sin? 'You said you couldn't believe that someone with such a good brain was going to take on all that claptrap you'd had to think your way out of – and only for artistic reasons. But you didn't say "artistic" you said something else.'

'Poetic, dramatic, aesthetic.'

Lex shook her head. She didn't remember. She hadn't had a religious education and she wanted to ask her father a question about original sin. She asked was it knowledge, not sex, that was the sin?

'No, it was disobedience,' the Historian said.

'He's a Presbyterian.' Lex's father jerked a thumb at the other man. 'And Presbyterians don't lapse, they just reach their fullest expression in leaving the church altogether. Don't mind him. It *is* sex. That was what God didn't want Adam and Eve to know about. He said, don't eat of that fruit. He was as worried about the fruit as the eating. Why do you want to know this, Lex?'

Lex couldn't figure out how to explain. In those stories about the early sins that set humankind off on the wrong course, until the crucifixion made a course-adjustment, there was never *one* sin but a many-headed cyst, like the carbuncle Frank had finally, impatiently, excised from his own leg, intact, with surrounding flesh. There was a first cause, then persistent poisoning. Adam and Eve, having eaten the forbidden fruit, should have faced God squarely, not hidden themselves. Cain killed Abel and hid the corpse, increasing the severity of his crime. Cain said: 'Am I my brother's keeper?' All the shame, secrecy and denial in these stories – that's what Lex wanted to ask about – what was the thinking about it, what was the scale, how did these sins compare?

Lex made a halting attempt to ask – and her father said that, in his book, murder was worse than fobbing God off.

The Historian said that a crime, without shame, and with no attempt to conceal it, was sometimes more an act of rebellion. If Cain had left Abel stinking in the field, then he'd have been saying to God: 'I haven't signed on for your laws.'

'Or, if Adam and Eve had been brassy instead of covered with shame,' Frank said, and the Historian finished, 'they would have been making it clear that, despite the fact God gave them everything, they didn't have to obey his mores.'

Lex knew that *mores* were morals, not eels. She noticed that the men had said 'laws' of murder and 'mores' about sex. Lex had always been encouraged to make distinctions between what was illegal and what immoral – for instance, all her family supported homosexual law reform. But somehow she was getting lost in these distinctions. All she wanted to understand was, of all the errors she had made, which was the worst? She'd just been told that, without shame, some crimes are acts of rebellion. Critchlow was shameless – but no hero. Yet if she hadn't been ashamed, she would have been able to tell the whole story, and be the hero Steph needed.

The man she scarcely knew, the Historian, said to her, 'You're too young to think about this.' Kindly.

Young, the sun of her understanding still on the ascendant. A sun that, at a low angle, shone through a forest of distinctions, making another forest of shadows – which lay like bars, a black cattle-stop, across her path.

10

On the first day of summer break Lex was on the flat lawn beneath the walnut tree, jumping. She had threaded her bamboo between two loop-headed steel stanchions, planted perhaps too close together. She had her doubts whether, if she did strike the bamboo, it would flex and pop free, rather than trip her. There wasn't time to move a stanchion, to hammer it into the lawn at the right height. Steph was still in her pyjamas. Steph was on the phone to a friend and would possibly soon finish her call.

Lex was jumping over her own head. As her feet left the ground, she closed up, her leading leg barging through thin air, her right leg following like a coat tail in a gale.

She came down so lightly that it seemed to her that there should be *more* to follow, as if she were a four-footed animal that had outrun its own hindquarters.

After a dozen jumps, on her way back to the runway, Lex caught sight of a child standing in the cropped grass of the paddock by Critchlow's orchard. The girl was around Steph's age, and wore a plaid skirt, a yellow skivvy with paler lemony kneesocks and Alice-band. The very different colour values between her clothes, and the dull grass and shady orchard, lent the girl the look of an apparition, as though the whole scene were a collage, and the girl a cut-out paper doll. But, when she moved, the child became three-dimensional. She climbed out of sight behind the Keenes' house.

Lex went to look. The paddock was full of people: three men, one woman and three children – two school age, and one a fair-haired tot. Two of the men stood at the top of the section, studying a plan. The third man was hammering wooden pegs into the ground.

Lex realised that the section had sold. Foundations were being measured, and these would be the new neighbours.

As Lex stood, partly concealed by a taupeta bush, she saw Steph appear on the footpath of Bayview Road, above the paddock. Steph saw the family, the architect, the builder. She slowed then stopped to look. Lex saw that her sister had *chanced* on this scene, hadn't come out just to see what was going on.

Lex left the fence, and ran around the house, up the steps, swinging under the branch. When she reached the road she saw that Steph had continued on uphill, and was nearly at Critchlow's gate. Lex called out to her.

Steph came back down. She seemed apprehensive, but at least met Lex's eyes.

'Where do you think you're going?'

Steph was going up Bayview Road to see her friend Callum. He had a new mouse. Together perhaps they could start a *mouse club*.

'Fine,' Lex said. She waved Steph on and stood watching until her sister disappeared down the driveway to Callum's. She waited. After a long interval Steph reappeared – saw Lex and hesitated, bumblefooted, missed a step, then came on down.

'Callum wasn't in.'

'Fine,' Lex said, again. She let her little sister walk past her, then closed in, herded Steph back down the steps and indoors.

Critchlow had made so great an inroad into Steph's routines, it seemed, that she was finding her visits a hard habit to shake. Perhaps in Critchlow Steph had found a kind of ally against sisters who neglected her and a mother who had failed to read her mind. Or perhaps Steph's compulsion was more a form of inertia. Steph was at a loose end, so she went up the road. Knotted her loose end around her own neck.

Lex had indigestion, a bubble trapped in her stomach, indigestible air foaming with swallowed spit. It was this that kept her awake and still until Steph was asleep and the house silent. A bottle of milk of magnesia was kept in a cupboard beside the laundry door. *Next to the back door.* Lex got up to medicate her sore stomach. She stood, her feet sticky on the cold lino, and uncapped the bottle. She took a teaspoon-sized sip, screwed the cap back on and put the bottle back in the cupboard.

She had decided – she let her thoughts follow her, out the back door, the key on the inside of its deadlock. Once the door was open Lex froze on the step, the key still in the lock, its oval head hard in her palm. She couldn't leave the door unlocked, the key on the inside. Someone might get up and, for some reason, check the lock, then lock her out. And the house couldn't be left unlocked, and her family exposed to an attack by stealth in the few minutes she was gone. Lex couldn't leave her family unless she knew they'd be safe. If she couldn't watch over them she would share their fate. The killing danger that Lex felt lay in wait outside the house every night now could have them all. It could tidy them all away but – please – not come while she was out, take them, and leave her alone.

(At this point, and with these thoughts, *another* person, not this girl standing in a porch in her nightdress, the key between her hand and the lock like a closed circuit, another person, with a gun to hand, might think of a *surer* way to put his imperilled loved ones out of harm's way. But this girl hadn't that sense of mastery or ownership.)

Lex removed the key from the lock and locked her family in. She sat down on the step to put on her gumboots. First she banged their heels against the step and shook them out, the usual precaution against any wetas seeking sanctuary from cats, who would carry them as far as the back door but then couldn't manage the cat flap. Lex remembered the cat flap. She pushed it open and placed the key on the floor just inside – where she could reach it when she came back – and where her family would find it if there was a fire.

Thinking on other sorts of danger, Lex had remembered fires.

Hester's yard broom had a loose handle. Lex had heard her mother cursing it when it fell apart while she was sweeping the path. Lex set one gumbooted foot on the broom's head and pulled the handle free.

She went up the steps to Bayview Road, hesitating while still under cover of the bottle-brush to look for headlamps lighting the reflective sign that warned of the tight bend at the far end of the cutting. There was no traffic. In the near houses no lights showed. The only motion was in the sky, where the stars seemed to seethe, as though seen through heat fuming from a smokeless fire.

Lex walked up the road, carefully raised the latch on Critchlow's gate and went through. She paused only a moment, to check for what she expected, the shape of the birdcage behind the kitchen window, the cage draped, the bird asleep. No reflection appeared in the black glass, no girl with a white face and white-knuckled hand around a club of broom handle. The nearest streetlamp was on the far side of the road and the night was at its fullest saturation. But Lex could see the broom handle, in silhouette, poised like a spear. She moved it away from the window beyond which the budgie was asleep, and went around the corner to the first row of windows on that wall. She tapped on one with the rounded end of the broom handle, watched the two blacks of night and reflected spear shiver. Then she hauled back and struck the glass. Its glossy darkness fell apart, and underneath was matte darkness. Lex went on to the next window, smashed it, then rained a series of hard, wasteful blows on the wall between those windows and the next, lost no momentum, broke another, watched the glass fly into the room.

There was a cry. 'Who is it?' It was a cry of pure dread.

Lex stopped. She went deaf. The glass skated underfoot. She bolted back through Critchlow's gate and was nearly at the head of her own steps when she saw the light go on in her living room.

She clambered over the fence, skidded down the bank beside the house, caught hold of the edge of the guttering at the house's blind corner and slipped between the retaining wall and the wall of the house. She abandoned the broom handle.

The woodbox next to the chimney had two small doors, one outside and one inside the house. The fireplace was in Frank's office, and it was hardly ever used, so there would be little or no kindling between the doors. When Lex was younger, the woodbox had been a secret escape hatch in childhood games. The Keene girls didn't let on to their friends; why betray such a great source of awe and surprise? *The captured rebel escapes though a guard is posted at the only door. A message has found its way to the imprisoned princess, though she was watched, her doors barred and windows screened.*

Lex pulled the door open on a square the size of a large atlas. To open the second door, which was at a right angle to the first, she pushed her head and shoulders into the woodbox. Her face caught a spider web and pulled it, whole, from its moorings. Lex opened the inside door. The curtained office was no less dark. One room away Lex heard a key being put to a lock. She heard her mother caution her father to be careful. Lex began to worm her way through the woodbox. She had grown. When her shoulders were through the second door her hips wedged in the first, between them her body bent at a cramped ninety degrees. She flexed her spine until, it seemed, her hips tripped the tumblers of a lock – an impossible fit – and she popped through the first door. Then thrashing and pushing she got a leg into the woodbox and shoved. Her nightdress caught and tore – then she slid all the way out onto the office floor.

Hester and Frank were outside, Hester under the clothesline and Frank speaking to her over the fence. Frank spoke as though he meant not to be overheard. He said that someone had broken Crit's windows. 'I'll go and see if he's all right, and whether he wants to call the police.'

'I suppose you should,' Hester said.

'I might be obliged to help him clean up a little.'

'Yes,' Hester said. Then she said, 'But Frank, please don't bring him back here.'

'No,' Frank said, and his tone was identical to his wife's – tired and wary.

Lex crept past the open back door, through the kitchen, and along the hall to her bedroom.

Steph was still fast asleep.

Lex got back into her bed. As her parents returned to bed, and their voices played out into silence, Lex lay awake. The tear in her nightgown was a vent for cold, for a cold hand resting lightly against her hip. She lay on the surface of sleep, her weight spread on its thin ice, broken at any moment, a jagged mouth with an airless interior.

*

On the evening Lex next set up her jump the light was poor. The air pressure had fallen and her body felt swollen and heavy. Over the lawn the air was contaminated by tiny bodies, the midges that Grace Hutton's mother called 'mayflies', as if making some excuse for them.

Lex stood back from the jump and pushed her eyes to focus on the bamboo, like a last buff strip of light on a flat horizon.

The jump failed. Lex misjudged. Her leading foot came down hard on the bar – her horizon – and broke it in two.

Afterword

When I was pregnant with my son Jack – now seven – I began writing *Pomare*. I saw it as a work in itself, and as a first instalment in a longer work. I had already written the second instalment, *Paremata*. I'm no George Lucas, and all I'll say about my having begun in the middle was that *that* was the order in which these stories ripened and fell off the tree into my hands.

Given my intention – to write three works, each complete in itself, and each part of a greater whole – I was heartened to find, as I revised them for this edition – *The High Jump* – that together *Pomare*, *Paremata* and *Tawa* are a novel, consistent in mood and metaphor and character. In fact, I was as much startled as heartened, because *The*

High Jump is autobiographical. How could I have imagined my life in so confidently consistent a way? Of course, *The High Jump* is autobiographical *fiction* – life with the application of imagination. I think that as soon as I began to make the decisions of a novelist – compressing the events of months into weeks, or the history of three years into one, or turning four people into two, or two into one – as soon as I started in with a novelist's maths and physics and chemistry, the events of my life began to yield up meanings with designs, with a designing eye behind them.

The three books in the order of their composition are a little history of my progress as a writer. *Paremata*, which I wrote in 1988, has that 'floating narrator' only to be found elsewhere in my work in the novel that I had set aside and would soon take up again, *Treasure*. And, although I abandoned that floater, I think it quite suits the drifting, paused, summer-holiday feel of *Paremata*. In *Pomare* I use a limited number of points of view (five). *Tawa*, which I wrote in the last months of 1997, while *The Vintner's Luck* was off in the world seeking a publisher, has only one point of view, Lex's. This was a considered decision. Because much of the whole project of *Tawa* is to show how disremembering, misinformation, assumption and avoidance can have tragic consequences, I had to settle the novella's eye in only one mind, the mind of a young person not equal to what she has to know and understand.

I have talked about these novellas during the years in which they appeared, and have, time and again, been asked questions about truth. It seems to me that questions about 'truth' in autobiography are questions about authority and openness. Authority – 'What makes you think you are the one to write about these things, which you don't solely own?' A good question, but only to *bear in mind*, because if it was acted on, negatively (who am I, after all?), then books about our life experiences would only ever be composed by committees of historians. Openness – well, openness is tricky, given the deep resources of contradiction in any human. I can only say I try to do my best, squinting my eyes against the brightness, trying to make a translation into sentences and stories of the vividness of things, to do what I hope *The High Jump* does – commemorate ordinary lives, the past, and say: 'These things are ours. These were the things we first learned to own.'

Elizabeth Knox
April 2000